SECRETS OF THE FISHING PROS

THE HUNTING & FISHING LIBRARY®

Edited by Dick Sternberg and Parker Bauer

DICK STERNBERG is a top fishing pro and Director of the *Hunting & Fishing Library* book series. These highly acclaimed how-to books have set the standard in the outdoor publishing field, and total sales currently number over one million copies.

PARKER BAUER began writing on fishing and the environment for national magazines while he was still in high school. He wrote the script for the award-winning documentary *Bigmouth*, a life history of the largemouth bass, and also helped film it.

CY DECOSSE INCORPORATED
Chairman: Cy DeCosse
President: James B. Maus
Executive Vice President: William B. Jones

SECRETS OF THE FISHING PROS
Hunting & Fishing Library Director and Contributing Writer: Dick Sternberg
Other Contributing Writers: Gerald Almy, Jake Barnes, Robert H. Boyle, Greg Breining, Nat Franklin Jr., Reinhold Gatz, Frank Sargeant
Editors: Parker Bauer, Dick Sternberg
Project Manager: Joseph Cella
Assistant Project Manager: Tracy Wright

Art Directors: Bradley Springer, Cy DeCosse, William B. Jones
Principal Photographer: William Lindner
Staff Photographers: Rex Irmen, Mark Macemon
Photo Directors: Joseph Cella, Ben Streitz
Photo Assistants: Mike Hehner, Jim Moynagh, Eric Lindberg, Tracy Wright, Robert Merila, Andy Lessin
Researchers: Robert Merila, Eric Lindberg, Ben Streitz
Production Manager: Jim Bindas
Assistant Production Managers: Julie Churchill, Jacquie Marx
Typesetting: Kevin D. Frakes, Linda Schloegel
Production Staff: Janice Cauley, Sheila DiPaola, Joe Fahey, Carol Kevan, Yelena Konrardy, Scott Lamoureux, Bob Lynch, David Schelitzche, Delores Swanson, Nik Wogstad
Illustrators: Jon Q. Wright, Thomas Boll
Contributing Photographers: Laurance Aiuppy, Gerald Almy, Lionel Atwill, Charlotte Bauer, Erwin Bauer, Florida Department of Natural Resources, Steve Grooms, Daniel Halsey, The In-Fisherman, Andy Lessin, Mark Miller, Frank Sargeant, South Florida Water Management District, Dick Sternberg, Ben Streitz
Cooperating Individuals and Agencies: Hiliary Bates; Jerry Bergin, Chippewa Pines Resort; Larry Bottrof, California Department of Fish & Game; Bright Waters, Inc.; Jim Brown, San Diego Water Utilities Department; Larry and Kathy Brunner; Burger Brothers Sporting Goods; Camp Fish; Ken Darwin, Michigan Fisherman; Peter DeGregorio, Dee's Bait & Tackle; Bubba Denton; John Edstrom; Mark Emery; Kelly Ferguson; Doug Fletcher, Washington Department of Wildlife, Fish Management Division; Butch Furtman; Doug Harper, National Marine Fisheries Service; Hill's Landing and Restaurant; Mark Hudy, Arkansas Game & Fish Commission; The In-Fisherman; T.J. Laviolette; Roger Lowden; Mike Maceina, South Florida Water Management District; Mike Miller; Ken Moore, White Hole Acres Resort; Brian Nelson, Florida Department of Natural Resources; Wally Pease, KYVE-TV, Yakima, Washington; John Phillips; R & R Marine; Roy's Live Bait; Scott Schumacher; Slim's Fish Camp; R.C. Smith; Tom Smith; Mike Snyder; Melissa Boucher, Ron Southwick, Virginia Department of Game & Inland Fisheries; Harold Staley; Colin Stass; Harry Styles; Thorne Brothers Custom Rod & Tackle; Rich Zaleski
Cooperating Manufacturers: Blue Fox Tackle Co.; Bomber Bait Company; Dura-Pak Corporation; Feldmann Eng. & Mfg. Co., Inc.; Fenwick/Woodstream; Hildebrant Corporation; Koden International, Inc.; LaCrosse Footwear, Inc.; Lowrance Electronics; Luhr Jensen & Sons, Inc.; Marine Metal Products Co., Inc.; Mercury Marine/Mariner Outboards; Micronar Electronics/Hondex Marine Electronics; Nordic Crestliner Boat Co.; Normark Corporation; Northland Tackle Co.; The Orvis Company, Inc.; Plano Molding Company; Storm Manufacturing Co.; Tru-Turn, Inc.; Wright and McGill Co.

Color Separations: ScanTrans
Printing: R.R. Donnelley & Sons, Co. (0289)

Also available from the publisher: *The Art of Freshwater Fishing, Cleaning & Cooking Fish, Fishing With Live Bait, Largemouth Bass, Panfish, The Art of Hunting, Fishing With Artificial Lures, Walleye, Smallmouth Bass, Dressing & Cooking Wild Game, Freshwater Gamefish of North America, Fishing Update No. I, Trout*

Contents

Introduction

Fishing is a sport that abounds with secrets — secret lures, secret techniques, secret spots. When someone shares one of these secrets with someone else, there is an implied understanding that the information remain just that — a secret.

Consequently, it's very difficult for the average fisherman to discover the secrets that enable a select few anglers to catch the majority of the fish. We've all heard the expression "ten percent of the fishermen catch ninety percent of the fish." Those figures have been confirmed by creel-census studies over the years; and as time goes on, the odds for the average angler will probably diminish even further. As fishing pressure increases, fish tend to become more "educated," so it takes more sophisticated techniques to catch them. In some heavily fished waters, it's likely that five percent of the fishermen now catch ninety percent of the fish.

The purpose of this book is to acquaint you with the little-known techniques that enable these highly skilled anglers to catch dozens or even hundreds of fish on days when the majority of fishermen come in skunked.

The first step in planning this book was to find out who the very best fishermen really are. To accomplish this, our research staff spent months talking to bait-shop operators, resort owners, game wardens, outdoor writers and anyone else knowledgeable about fishing in their region. We compiled a list of highly recommended anglers, then talked to each one to determine "the best of the best."

We soon discovered that the most successful anglers are not necessarily the most famous. Many of the pros featured in this book make their living as guides and spend almost every day on the water. When the TV fishing stars come to town, they often hire these pros to help them catch fish for their shows.

After making our final selections, we arranged to send writers and photographers on trips with each pro, study his methods in detail, and prepare an in-depth article for the book.

The articles are organized into chapters covering every major category of freshwater fish: Largemouth and Smallmouth Bass, Walleye and Sauger, Northern Pike and Muskellunge, Panfish, and Trout and Salmon. There's even a catchall chapter that includes striped bass, catfish, and a mixed bag of saltwater species.

In the course of our research, we talked to hundreds of other fishing experts in addition to the featured pros. Many offered tips that were highly useful, but did not warrant a complete article in the book. Rather than ignore this valuable information, we incorporated the best tips into a special section at the end of each chapter. Many of these tips involve little things, like doctoring lures or modifying rigs, but they can make a tremendous difference in catching fish.

Secrets of the Fishing Pros is a book brimming with detailed how-to fishing information, most of which has rarely, if ever, been seen in print. We're confident you'll find it an invaluable reference. Even though the featured pros may fish on other waters in other parts of the country, the techniques they use can be adapted to many of the waters that you fish.

Largemouth & Smallmouth Bass

Big 'Dads = Big Bass

by Frank Sargeant

Bill Murphy, the all-time "teen bass" champion, considers crawdads the deadliest bait

T he object of Bill Murphy's passion came to California some 25 years ago. That's when the first largemouths of the Florida subspecies were transplanted to the deep impoundments that dot the mountains east of San Diego. The Florida bass took to the strange environment with a vengeance, feeding on hordes of shad and golden shiners, and even on fingerling trout the state had planted in most of the lakes. With the abundant food and the insulating, highly oxygenated depths, the bass grew and fed year round.

By the early 1970s, trophies were being turned out on a regular basis. In a few years more, state records began to topple as monstrous bass showed up in numbers unheard of anywhere else in the country. The little lakes, most less than 5 miles long, became national catchwords: Otay, San Vincente, Casitas, and El Capitan. Less well-known, but also productive, were Marino, Barrett, Hodges, Sutherland, Henshaw, Murray, Jennings, Miramar, Poway, Dixon, Skinner, Wohlford, and Vail.

Murphy was in the vanguard devising techniques for taking the giants now lurking in these lakes — techniques that eventually produced four of the six International Gamefish Association line-class reccords, including the second-largest bass of all time, a 21-pound 3-ounce behemoth caught by Ray Easley in 1980.

Bill Murphy

Home: *Santee, California*

Occupation: *Dental technician*

In southern California, in the world of big bass, Bill Murphy has earned the nickname "Lunker Bill." Over the last twenty years, from the desert reservoirs around San Diego, he's regularly caught some of the largest bass in the nation.

The red-bearded Irishman extracts these giants with a skill, patience, and attention to detail learned in his job as a dental technician. Sometimes, in fashioning his own tackle, he even employs the same tools he uses in making dental plates for San Diego dentists.

Murphy gained fame by trolling Magnum Rapalas, hand-painted with up to twenty coats to precisely match the rainbow trout forage. He used lead-core line, as much as 200 feet, carrying the lures as deep as 70 feet to hook lunkers untouched by shallower fishing techniques. Another of his methods is fishing homemade giant plastic worms. Some of his worms measure 16 inches long.

But for most of his fishing, Murphy now uses a different method: anchoring and slowly retrieving live crawfish. He feels this technique takes the biggest bass.

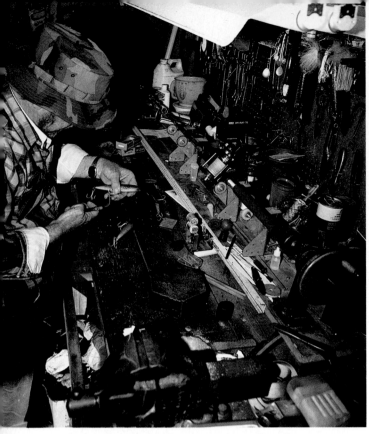

At his workbench, Murphy customizes a trolling plug

Murphy's Rapalas, hand-painted to mimic bass forage

Murphy himself has boated 38 bass over 13 pounds, including eight over 15 pounds; his biggest is 16 pounds 15 ounces. This probably makes him the all-time champion of what he calls "teen" fish — the only bass that get him excited.

Bill has lived here twenty years, and the wood of his workbench is burnished black with the continual rubbing of his big forearms as he labors on yet another refinement to yet another custom lure. The early models of his painted Rapalas hang here, now layered with dust. Some wear two dozen coats of translucent paint, laid on over weeks to achieve the living glow of a young trout. The hook points of each have been perfectly triangulated — under the same microscope Murphy uses to perfect the dentures he makes in his lab.

Murphy still trolls with Rapalas in the dead of winter, and says the technique is superb for locating fish. He uses lead-core line, sometimes 200 feet of it, to reach the deep winter haunts of the big bass.

Piled in every corner of the workshop are plastic worms in wild shapes and colors, all designed and poured by Murphy. His worm molds are masterworks, evidence of the skill with tiny tools that has made him a widely sought dental technician. There's the mold for a lead-bodied spinner he calls the Little Murph: he cast it in one of the denture furnaces at his office from old pennies. Lures from this mold look as if they were struck in a coin mint — perfect in every detail.

There are a host of good fishermen around San Diego, a coterie of giant-bass anglers who know each other and keep tabs on each other's catches — but who never, never fish together.

"Only one captain per boat," says Murphy. "Each of us wants to give the orders."

These are incredibly patient men, willing to fish a full day, or even several days, for a single bass. They are comparable to muskie fishermen, to marlin fishermen — and maybe even more so to deer hunters. In fact, Murphy calls one of the techniques he's developed "stand hunting," because he takes a stand and waits there in absolute silence for his giant prey to come to him, the same way he'd await a ten-point whitetail.

"Really big bass survive because they're wary," says Murphy. "They're like trophy bucks, because if they observe the slightest thing that's unusual in their habitat, they won't bite. Remember, these fish have spent maybe eight to twelve years in the same general vicinity, so they know how every rock and twig looks, just what the natural sounds are, and what foods they should find there. It's like a chess game; the challenge is to avoid making a bad move. I don't care if I land them — I release them all now, anyway — but fooling a big one is checkmate."

Murphy says he has been successful because he's willing to set up on a big-fish spot and wait until

For years, Murphy's giant bass have kept writers and photographers busy at southern California newspapers

everything returns to normal, so the bass aren't aware of his presence. He looks for rocky points or rubble piles that rise within 15 feet of the surface but drop away sharply, sometimes down to 100 feet of water.

Some of this structure has weed growth, but the usual form of cover is rubble or decaying brush and trees. The biggest bass, Murphy says, have no predators to hide from and require just enough cover to camouflage themselves from their prey. In the really thick cover, only the smaller bass are likely to hang out.

He fishes from a 15-foot aluminum semi-V with a 25-horsepower outboard and a transom-mounted electric motor. The boat's interior is padded from

Murphy's no-frills bass rig, an aluminum semi-V

bow to stern with thick carpet. Under the hand-fitted floorboards, poured flotation muffles the noise of waves slapping the hull. Murphy poured it himself to make sure there were no voids to create a drum effect. Carpet is fitted on the inner sides of the boat, to quiet the scraping of rods there when he takes them out of the racks or replaces them. His flasher and graph recorder are mounted on the middle seat.

Also, Murphy has designed and welded up a pair of enormous, multi-clawed steel anchors, each attached to 100 feet of line, which let him rivet the boat over the deep rockpiles and points where he most often finds the giants. "If the anchor goes bouncing through the rocks, you can forget it," he advises. "Noise like that shuts them down every time."

Before he starts fishing, he graphs an area carefully, studying each of the inverted *V* marks that represent fish. With years of experience under his belt, he feels he can tell the approximate size of a fish by the thickness of the mark it makes on the graph paper.

Once he's settled into his "stand," Murphy rarely uses his electric motor, and he keeps the depth finders turned off. "Electronics create noise in the water. I can hear it — and if I can, you know the fish can. They may not spook, but they're less inclined to feed when you're zapping them with sound pulses."

Murphy deposits his night's catch into his crawdad tank

Marking a craw for color-selective bass

Murphy's favorite bait for the warmer months, spring to fall, is now live crawdads. "In all our lakes 'dads are a natural food, and they're easy for us to catch and keep," says Murphy. In two giant tanks outside his home he stores about a thousand, replenishing them with weekly forays to neighborhood ditches after dark.

When Bill heads for the lake, he takes up to 15 dozen 'dads with him. He keeps a snapping carpet of them in two ice chests, adding an inch of water to keep them happy, segregating them by size so the big ones don't eat the little ones.

Reaching into the box is like reaching into a rattlesnake den. Every crawfish in there rears back, pincers poised like pointed boxing gloves. Some look like miniature — but not very miniature — lobsters. When you get hold of a crawfish — quickly grabbing it by the back of the shell before an adjacent 'dad can nail you — you pull it out and catch it by one of the claws.

Murphy says it's smart to remove one pincer so that the crawfish isn't such a formidable bite for the bass: "A 13-pounder can gobble up the biggest crawfish there is, but if it's got both claws he has to whip its butt first. With one claw, the crawfish just tries to escape when a bass approaches, and that turns on the fish's attack instinct." To remove a claw, you simply crack the shell of it. The crawfish will then activate its escape mechanism, neatly detaching the arm from its body. The craw isn't permanently damaged: if released, it will quickly grow a new pincer.

At times, Murphy uses some unusual tricks to make his 'dads more appealing to the bass. He's found that bass in different lakes prefer different colors, so he paints his 'dads with waterproof

markers, some of which come in two-tone colors like silver and green or silver and blue.

Another secret is to treat his crawdad hooks and the first few inches of his line with a special potion, to conceal his scent. He mixes cod-liver oil, anise, vanilla, saccharin, salt, and even anti-freeze in a mineral oil base, varying the proportions from season to season.

Home-brewed potion on hook and line masks human scent

Murphy fishes the crawfish unweighted. In sparse cover, he uses an Eagle Claw 139 Baitholder hook in size 4; in thicker stuff, a Mustad 9174 in size 6 with the bend opened slightly. The line is 6- to 12-pound mono, depending on the clarity of the water. He uses lines in various tints, to match the water color as it changes through the seasons. In summer, when the water has a green color from suspended algae, he uses a line with a greenish tint. In fall and winter, when the algae dies off and the water clears, he prefers line with a grayish tint or clear line. Trophy bass are definitely line-shy, Murphy says.

For angling from late spring through early fall, the hook goes through the "horn" at the front of the crawfish's shell. Inserted here, squarely between the eyes, the hook hits no vital parts. The crawfish can survive for hours, and if it doesn't get eaten, can be returned to the home tank where the hook hole will soon heal shut. Also, a craw hooked this way will dive faster to the productive depth, and can be fished in a single spot more easily: it pulls away from the angler, so he can retrieve it a little and then let it swim out again.

In the cooler months, he hooks the craws through the tail, in the second segment from the tip. The hook must be inserted to the side of the tail vein, not in the vein itself, or the craw will be killed. Tail-hooking conceals the hook better, so it helps deceive cautious bass in the clear water of winter. Lighter line can be used, since a tail-hooked craw is easier to pull through cover without snagging.

A crawdad hooked in the horn usually swims hard straight down, so it's no problem to hit bottom even in 20 to 40 feet of water, the depths Murphy likes to fish early in the summer. In Florida, the ancestors of these fish never visited such deep water haunts — Florida lakes are shallow — but in California lakes the fish thrive in the deepest depths, preferring them to the shoreline all year, except briefly during the spawn.

Murphy fishes the crawdads with an excruciatingly slow retrieve. He gathers short coils of line in his hand, as though retrieving a fly line. "I want to know exactly what's going on down there," he says. "If you run the line directly to the reel, you can't feel it. Sometimes these fish just suck the bait in and hold it a second, and if they feel the slightest line pressure, they spit it. If I retrieve by hand, I know when they take."

Murphy's hands-on crawdad retrieve

How Murphy Rigs Crawfish for Giant Bass

REMOVE one pincer by crushing it with pliers. The craw has an internal mechanism which then detaches the entire arm. Pulling it off would kill the craw.

HOOK the craw through the "horn" on the head for warm-weather fishing. Hooked this way, it will dive rapidly to reach bass holed up in the cool depths.

INSERT the hook through the second segment of the tail for cold-weather bass. This conceals it better, an advantage in the clear water of wintertime.

13

Bill fishes the baits on 7-foot spinning rods he's built himself. The rods are jointed, the lower section made from a heavy saltwater spinning blank, the top from a much softer freshwater blank. The combination of sections gives plenty of flex to make long casts with the bait, yet lots of authority to control the fight. The reels are seasoned saltwater spinning models, chosen for their large spools — an advantage in casting light baits because the line peels off with less friction.

Fishing for big bass is normally a slow, painstaking proposition, but Bill has sometimes boated more than 100 in a day while using 'dads. "A few years back, I think it was in October, I caught over 100 bass a day for three days straight," Bill recalls. "They all came from the same spot. It was a rocky hump that topped off at 11 feet. The bass were hitting before the bait ever reached bottom. Nothing really huge, but I had an 11-4, a 9-15, and dozens over 7. They planted rainbows on the third day and that was the end of it. The bass scattered to feed on the trout."

While 'dads now account for most of Murphy's bass, some of his very biggest ones have been caught on plastic worms. In summer and winter, he uses 6- to 7¼-inch worms. A 7¼-incher also works well in spring and fall, but he often uses bigger worms then — much bigger. He can't buy worms big enough, so he molds his own, up to 16 inches long. "Worm" may not be the right term for a lure this size; "snake" would be better. His favorite colors are green, root beer, chocolate, blue

and black. He treats his worms with the potion mentioned earlier.

The retrieve is very slow, much like the one he uses with crawfish. When a fish hits, he gives it slack, reels in his excess line, then lets the fish pull the rod tip down before setting the hook. This way, the line is sure to be tight.

"My partner and I were fishing a tournament on Wohlford Lake some years back," Bill reminisces, "and we hadn't caught a single keeper all day. We had one spot left to try, but a boat was anchored up right where we wanted to fish. They weren't really fishing — it looked like they were all asleep, so we decided to give it a try.

"On the first cast, I moved my worm about 6 inches and she hit. When I set the hook, she tore away, leaped clear out of the water, then headed back toward the boat and swam around the anchor rope. I had to dunk my rod in the lake to get it around the rope, but we finally landed her. She weighed 15 pounds 9 ounces."

That single fish was enough to win the tournament. At that time, it was the largest bass ever caught in a fishing tournament, and it may still be.

The locals were duly impressed. If you look at the official Wohlford Lake brochure, you'll see the spot where Bill caught the fish. It's now designated as Murphy's Rock.

Anyone who can win a tournament with one fish deserves to have a spot named after him.

An Assortment of Murphy's Favorite Worms

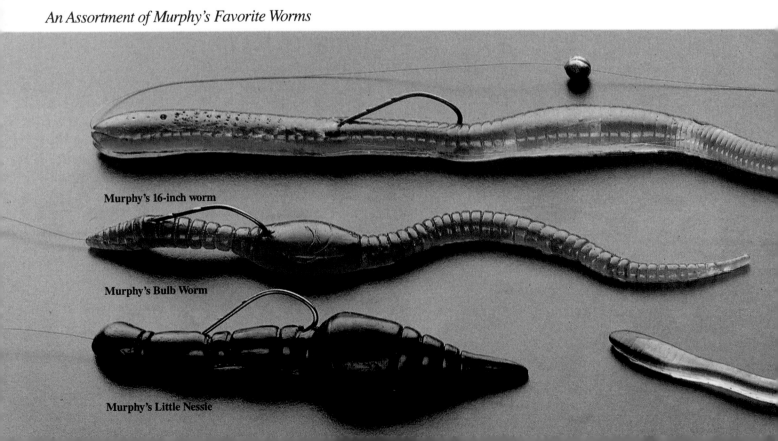

Murphy's 16-inch worm

Murphy's Bulb Worm

Murphy's Little Nessie

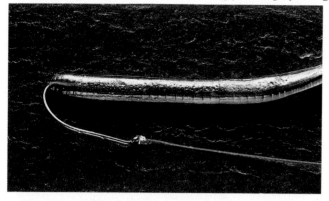

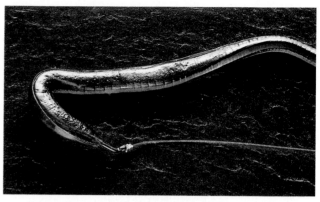

1. PUSH the point of an Eagle Claw 181 Baitholder hook, 1/0 or 2/0, into the head of the worm. Murphy flattens the shank barbs to avoid snagging debris.

2. THREAD the hook through the center of the plastic. Work the hook farther along the length of the worm than you would in rigging Texas-style.

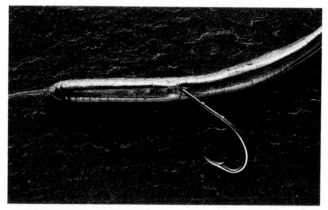

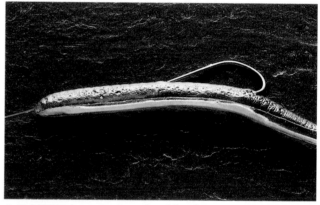

3. BRING the hook out of the worm, 1 to 3 inches from the head; leave the eye embedded. With the hook this far back, bass are less likely to feel it.

4. INSERT the point into the side of the worm, not deep in the center. The offset hook should point out for best hooking. Add a split-shot about 5 inches up the line.

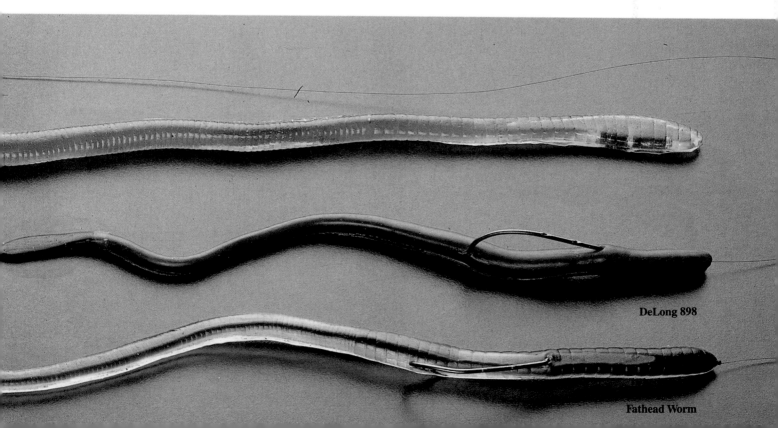

DeLong 898

Fathead Worm

Spoon-Fed Largemouths

by Frank Sargeant

Using a weedless spoon, Lance Glaser covers lots of water to locate elusive Florida bass

Lance Glaser attracted plenty of attention when he blew into the black-dirt town of Belle Glade, Florida, in 1975, and announced he was going to be a bass guide on Lake Okeechobee.

Not only were the local residents skeptical about his bass-catching capabilites, they were somewhat taken aback by his outspoken demeanor. Most of his ideas and opinions came from his experience as a blue-water charterboat captain in Hawaii.

"God gave you two hands," Glaser told anybody who would listen — including plenty of guides who hadn't asked. "Why use a rod designed for one?"

You won't find one of those "contemptible" one-hand baitcasting or spinning rods in his boat — or in a lot of other bass boats these days. But way back then, it was heresy to speak against the pistol grip.

He had plenty of other ideas that didn't quite sit right with locals — including the suspicion that flying saucers were not, in fact, bunk. "We don't talk to ants," he told me and numerous other folks as we had lunch in a lakeside restaurant a while back. "Why should a civilization with the capability to travel light years to visit here talk to us?"

There's no denying that Lance Glaser is different. He dresses like a rodeo cowboy, he sings Yiddish songs of praise to ask for a bit of help from above when the fish won't bite — and sometimes he dresses them down with a string of epithets if they don't respond.

Glaser's living habits are different, too. On arrival in Belle Glade, he took up residence in a house-boat anchored near Slim's, a careworn fish camp on Kreamer Island. He quickly rounded up a troop

Lance Glaser

Home: *Belle Glade, Florida*

Occupation: *Largemouth bass guide on Lake Okeechobee*

Lance Glaser is one of the best-known guides on a lake that has hundreds of them. In 1975, Glaser came to Florida from Hawaii, to sample the fishing for the big Florida bass he had read about. Since then, he's never left — and says he never will.

Glaser has established a formidable reputation as a bass catcher. He routinely boats thirty or more bass a day when the weather is right, and on a few magical trips his daily catches have reached close to the 200 mark. He's also taken plenty of big bass, once carrying home a stringer of 20 fish that scaled 150 pounds and included several over 9 pounds each. That catch came in winter, on live wild shiners — which are almost a guarantee, he says, of a fish over 7 pounds at that time of year. But his biggest Okeechobee bass ever, a 13-pound 9-ounce hulk, came on his favorite lure — the weedless spoon.*

started listening to the fishing gospel according to Glaser.

To keep his customers in fish, Glaser employs a varied strategy, swimming giant shiners around the weeds in winter, dropping jigging spoons, plastic worms, and crankbaits over offshore holes and rock piles in summer. But his favorite tactic is to run a weedless spoon through the endless cover of the "Big O." He's made an art of it, refining his gear and approach and becoming one of the nation's best with this lure.

"The spoon has a big advantage over the plastic worm because it's a 'fast' bait," says Lance. "If you don't know where the fish are, you can cover acres of really thick cover just as fast as you can throw and reel. It's four or five times faster at covering the water than a worm, and in the active periods when I fish the spoon — spring and fall — the bass are ready to hit the faster-moving lure."

Glaser says that in Okeechobee, as in many large, fertile lakes, the bass move around in sizeable schools. Successful anglers search for these schools, not for individual stragglers. This means they have to cover the water rapidly.

"There's an awful lot of places where the fish ain't," as Glaser likes to put it.

But most good bass cover is so thick that few lures other than the Texas-rigged plastic worm will penetrate — and the worm is a slow bait. The spoon is both completely weedless and extremely fast.

"I fish the spoon from late February into June, and again from mid-September until the first cold front in late November or December," Glaser says. "The best time for it differs in other parts of the country, but there's a long period in spring and fall on every lake when the fish are in shallow water, around heavy cover. The spoon is the best locator bait you can choose for those conditions.

"If the water is high," he adds, "the bass will stay in shallow cover for a longer time in spring, before moving deep for the summer. High water in fall will bring them into the thick, shallow weeds earlier than usual; they don't stay so long in the sparser stuff on the deeper outside edges.

"If the water is low, the bass move out earlier in the spring. And they stay longer in the sparse outside cover in the fall, waiting for the water to rise before moving shallower."

Most often, Glaser fishes the Johnson Silver Minnow in the ½-ounce size. The gold and silver finishes are his favorites for bright days, black for dark days. He says these heavy metal lures need a bit of extra attention to do the job right.

of wildlife friends including some fifty raccoons that sat on the porch like masked pelicans, always awaiting a handout.

His wife eventually tired of the coons and a husband who always arose before dawn and never came home until after dark: Glaser was guiding as many as 300 days a year. She moved out. And a fire left the raccoons and Glaser homeless a few months back.

"It doesn't matter," says Glaser. "So long as I can fish, I got no problems."

He now rents a tiny duplex apartment, its yard jammed with bass boats, its porch knee-deep in tackle. Inside, the walls are covered with mounted trophy bass and endless racks of rods. Stacks of tackle boxes, boat props, minnow buckets, and rainsuits line the closets. His entire life, he says, revolves around fishing. He suspects a dead mouse behind the refrigerator, but has no time to worry about it. Except on nights when he squires select Belle Glade belles, he falls into bed at 9; he rises at 4, and spends nearly every waking minute either on the water or at Slim's.

It took years — and some remarkable stringers of bass — before the locals accepted him and actually

"First, give your spoons a test cast to make sure they don't spin. Very few of them do, but once in a great while you'll get one. If the lure spins, you'll need a swivel; and if you use a swivel, it will catch in the grass. So when you get one that spins, clip the line and give it the 'float test' — just throw it overboard."

Glaser admits that it might be possible to correct spoons that have a slight bend in the eye or an offset hook that causes them to spin, but he prefers not to fool with them.

On good spoons — the ones that wobble rather than spin — Glaser turns the hook point outward with a pair of pliers. He opens the gap until the point catches on his palm when dragged across it flat. "If the hook won't catch on your hand, it won't catch on a fish," he cautions.

He then sharpens the point on a small, grooved stone, until the tip is sharp enough to catch in his fingernail under the slightest pressure. Next he bends the wire weedguard outward a bit, so there's a half-inch of space between it and the hook point.

"When a bass wants the spoon, he just destroys it — *balooey*. He'll eat weeds, lily pads, whatever gets in the way. That extra space around the weed-guard won't keep you from getting the hook set — no way. But it keeps weeds clear that would otherwise catch, especially with the bend in the hook

opened up." To the hook, he attaches a twin-tail grub or some other grub with dual curved tails, pushing its head onto the hook point and upward against the body of the spoon. The tails lie flat, on the same plane as the spoon body. He uses yellow tails for gold spoons, white tails for silver, and black for black spoons.

"The twin tails provide more planing surface than a single tail," says Glaser. "That makes it easier to 'skim' the lure when you need to — just sliding it along right on the top — or to 'bulge' with it, running it just under the surface to form a slight hump in the water. And because the tails are short, they don't get snagged in weeds like a longer tail does. The two of them working together give the lure lots of action."

When the weeds are coated with sticky filaments of algae, he sometimes adds worm oil. This is not for the scent, but for the lubrication — which helps the soft-plastic tail slip through tight spots where it would otherwise pick up the algae or wrap around weed stems. One squirt lasts for ten minutes or so, he's found.

Glaser uses a long rod, usually a two-handed bait-caster, so he can power out long casts. He prefers heavy line, 15-pound test or better, because the long ranges sometimes involved in spoon fishing make it hard to set the big single hook with anything lighter.

How Glaser Fine-Tunes a Weedless Spoon

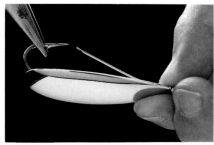

BEND the hook point outward slightly with pliers. By opening the gap, you improve your hooking percentage.

TEST the hook by pulling it across your palm. If the point catches, the gap is bent open wide enough.

SHARPEN the hook on a grooved stone. Sharpness is vital, since the big single hook can be difficult to set.

BEND the weedguard out to decrease snagging. Allow a half inch of space between the guard and hook point.

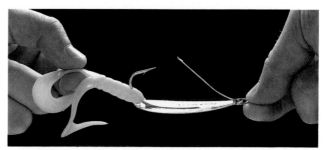

ATTACH a twin-tail grub. Align the tails with the plane of the spoon body to add lift to the lure.

WEEDS shown here make especially good cover for largemouths. Look for (1) maidencane, also known as panic grass; (2) Illinois pondweed; (3) hydrilla; (4) eelgrass, also known as tapegrass; (5) bulrushes and other rushes; (6) lotus pads. Edges where two of these different types meet are especially productive.

"You get a lot of stretch with light line, so that cuts your hook-setting force. And if you hook a fish, you need plenty of line strength to pull him through the weeds."

Glaser says the secret of avoiding snags with the spoon is to get it moving the instant it hits the water. "If you wait until the bait sinks to put the reel into gear, you'll pick up dreck half the time, and a fish will rarely hit if there's any vegetation on the lure. You have to be in gear and start reeling right away to keep it clean."

In Glaser's system, the spoon is a "place" lure. He doesn't tie it on and just fish it all day regardless of the cover, but instead he reserves it for areas where he knows it's likely to catch fish. These productive areas include beds of Illinois pondweed, hydrilla, eelgrass, scattered bulrushes and other rushes, maidencane, and lotus. The bottom depth will run from 3 to 5 feet.

He seeks areas where the bass just get fleeting glimpses of the lure as it moves through openings in the vegetation, rather than a good, clear look at it. "The weedless spoon isn't a realistic-looking bait. If a fish has a chance to study it in the open, he's not too likely to take it. But if he just gets a quick look at all that wobble and flash and squirming tail, a lot of the time he'll come right up through the cover to kill it — *kerpow.*"

Glaser says that edge cover, where two types of vegetation come together, is often highly productive.

"Run the lure right down the seam, where there's a little natural break only a foot or so wide, and more often than not you'll connect."

The areas he likes best have hard sand bottoms. Locations with very soft muck bottoms seldom hold bass. "Stay away from the common water lily we call bonnets here in Florida," he advises. "It looks good, but down here it grows in soft muck, not sand. Lotuses, those dinner-plate pads that grow above the water a foot or so — they grow on fairly hard bottoms, so they're good."

He also looks for areas where baitfish gather close to cover. "You don't see shad right up in the weeds," he says, "but if you find them working in a little bay with good weed cover around the edges, hammer that cover. I think bass rest in the weeds, then go out and work on the shad in the open water from time to time. Small bass schooling on the surface — the fish that produce the fastest action — usually feed on shad."

Glaser likes the silver spoon as a shad imitation for these smaller bass. But when he's after larger fish, he usually opts for the gold one. "It imitates a golden shiner, I guess, and that's what the big fish feed on when they're up in the shallows. Fish that gold one around spawning areas in spring as they're coming off the beds, and sometimes you'll wear them out."

Usually he fishes a steady retrieve; but when the lure comes to a hole in the grass, he hesitates momentarily and allows the spoon to glide toward bottom, rubber legs wiggling madly.

"Keep the rod down, pointed at the lure like a rifle, even when you slow down," he advises. "If the rod is high, you don't have anyplace to go with your hook set. If you're pointed at the lure when the strike comes, you have plenty of room to hit the fish. And remember, bass may come up on the bait anywhere — I've seen them blow right through stuff it looks like you could walk across."

He advises clients never to set the hook as soon as they see the splash of a fish rising to the bait. "The only time to set is when you feel the strike. They'll throw water all over the place and not have hold of the lure, but when you feel the hit you know you've got them."

There are times when fish are boiling at a spoon but not connecting, because the retrieve is too fast. But in many kinds of vegetation, the spoon will catch if slowed down and allowed to drop beneath the surface. Glaser solves the problem by attaching the shaft and blade of a Snagless Sally in-line spinner ahead of the spoon. The turning blade increases the water resistance of the lure, keeping it on top at the slower speed. It's useful in dirty water as well, giving fish some flash and vibration to home in on.

Keeping the lure from snagging can also be a matter of which direction you cast it. "Most vegetation aligns with the wind. Always fish with the grain of the windblown weeds, not across it, or you'll be snagged all the time."

Casting downwind with the grain is good, but casting upwind with it is usually better. That way, the stems of the vegetation lean toward you, and your

BUILD a spoon-spinner combination by removing the blade and beaded shaft from a Snagless Sally (top), then clipping them to a weedless spoon (bottom). The combo gives extra lift for slow surface retrieves.

spoon will swim through more easily. Also, Glaser says, "If you hit a school, and you're blowing down on them, you have less control — you'll get too close. But if you're downwind, you can hang out at the edge of casting range with your electric motor and work them better."

In addition, he suggests being careful where the line falls after a cast. If you bring it down between crossed reeds or into the notch of a pad, the spoon is sure to get stuck when it arrives there. By dropping the line to one side or the other, you avoid such snags.

How well does all this theory work? My last visit to Okeechobee was a prime example. I needed a bass for photos, in a hurry. I was on my way to a conference farther south, and had little time to spare. Could Glaser come up with a big one on short notice? "No problem," was his response.

We left the dock, ran five miles in five minutes, made no more than a dozen casts, and I reeled in a 6-pounder.

Glaser seems to have a knack for producing on demand. Consider, for instance, the time he had a local TV crew out on the lake with him: what they wanted was some turbulent action, right now, to compete with the A-Team and the drug busts on the evening Eyewitness News. For openers, he levered a 4-pounder out of the maidencane and swooshed it right up to the waiting lens. The cameraman bent to his work, Glaser boating and reboating the dazed fish numerous times.

Shortly afterward, casting again, Glaser had a good boil at his spoon. He jerked the lure away — deliberately — before the bass could chomp down on it. Hopping around, he explained everything: rare photo opportunity, don't miss it, here's what you do. Moments later, the TV host was stationed amidships doing an on-camera intro. Glaser fired out a cast on cue, and the camera followed the long arc of the spoon and its path across the water as he cranked it back in.

The chrome flashed and the tails wiggled, and when the right spot was reached a prodigious bass cleared the water completely, tumbled, and sucked in the spoon during re-entry. After that, the fish could shove nothing but its head above water — it was just too heavy. It plowed across the surface three separate times, head out, and then Glaser swung it aboard, sheets of water emptying from its gill flaps.

He weighed the bass for the shaking cameraman: 11½ pounds. The TV host, beside himself, had forgotten how to host. Glaser let out a whoop. The whole thing was in the can.

Rx for Fly-Rod Bass

by Nat Franklin Jr.

Jimmy Nix, pharmacist turned fly-fishing pro, mixes powerful medicine for Texas largemouths

In Texas, the heart of lunker-largemouth territory, fly fishing is such an anomaly that curious baitcasters drop their Shimanos and draw near for a look when Jimmy Nix hits the water. "Only one day out of a thousand," says Nix, "will I see someone besides me fly-fishing for bass on a Texas reservoir."

If that doesn't change — and soon — the blame won't belong to Nix. On weekends every spring and fall, at two ranches in east Texas, he conducts his own schools on fly fishing for bass. He also travels around the country to present seminars on the subject. The theme of all these sessions is that

fly angling is not only the most challenging method for bass but also the most enjoyable, if only your tackle and technique are up to snuff.

Recently, I spent a few days fishing with Nix. He met me at the Dallas airport on a 105-degree morning in June, and we headed for Lake O' the Pines in East Texas — an Army Corps of Engineers reservoir built in the 1950s for flood control. We arrived at the lake in midafternoon.

At that moment, a bit of flooding would have been welcome: the summer weather had been some of the driest in history. In front of the Willow Point Marina, a dried slab of mud temporarily marked the spot where the lake-record bass, 10 pounds 6 ounces, was dragged out. Nix wiped sweat from his forehead with his cap. He said the fishing was going to be tough, because of the heat and low water.

Five o'clock: lessening heat, or at least the illusion. At half throttle Nix heads his jonboat out a shallow channel. The boat is a 17-footer, broad-beamed, with a 50-horse outboard and a bow-mount electric. He's removed the swivel seats that came with the boat, so anglers can stand and cast with no obstructions for loose fly lines to get caught on. The electric motor sees minimal use; Nix is convinced its sound will spook fish, especially when the propeller bumps tough weed stems.

He swings out of the channel and creeps across a stretch of gray-brown water. Abruptly the bow aims skyward; the boat slides halfway over something unseen and hangs up, wobbling like a vulture perched in a windstorm. Pine stump: relic of a vast pre-reservoir woodland. "I've never had a crisis," says Nix. Opening the throttle, he heaves his shoulders from side to side. The hull shudders loose. Moments later he cuts the motor: the boat drifts near a nodding bed of lotuses.

These pads are where he expects to score. During April and May, the post-spawn period, the bass have been scattered through the deeper, open water down the lake and in channels here in the upper end; now, however, they should be moving among

---

Jimmy Nix

Home: *Farmers Branch, Texas*

Occupation: *Fishing instructor; sales representative for fly-tackle and outdoor-clothing companies*

Jimmy Nix has actually gone out and done what countless other anglers only dream of. One day in the summer of 1986, he took a deep breath and quit his secure, long-time profession — he was a pharmacist — and set out to earn a living somehow from fishing.

Now he spends much of his time traveling around the country to teach seminars in fly angling and fly tying. He also works in Texas and nearby states as a sales rep for manufacturers of fly rods, fly lines, flies, and sportswear designed for — who else? — fly fishermen. Another current project is a book: he's setting down on paper his years of hard-won personal knowledge on tying and fishing bass flies.

Nix has designed many innovative fly patterns which look and perform like the most important foods of bass, and are sure to become standards in the years ahead. He's written articles on these patterns for fly-tying magazines, and made a two-hour video titled Tying Bass Flies with Jimmy Nix. *Some of his patterns are tied commercially and are available through mail-order fly-tackle catalogs.*

Nix spent his early years in Oklahoma, starting to fly-fish at age nine. He won his first fly rod in an angling derby — an odd prize, since "the only fly fishermen I

knew of in the state of Oklahoma were my father and his fishing partner, Lloyd Cole." Later, his father would take him fishing on farm ponds near home; and whenever his father tied flies, he would sit for hours watching raptly. But those dream days came to an end too soon. When Nix was only thirteen, his father died. "I think that's why fly fishing means so much to me now," he says.

American lotus at Lake O' the Pines

the shallow pads, where a fly fisherman can present his offerings far more easily and effectively.

Nix thinks big when rigging up. For most of his bass fishing he uses a 9-foot, 9-weight Sage RP rod, a very stiff graphite. Sometimes he moves up to a 10-weight for the biggest flies: 3/0 or 4/0 divers. With floating lines he uses a simplified leader having only two sections, joined by a surgeon's knot. The butt, about two-thirds of the leader length, is .021- or .023-inch mono; the tippet is 12-pound Maxima, a very stiff but abrasion-resistant material that holds up well in heavy vegetation. With sinking lines he uses a 4- or 5-foot leader, untapered, 12-pound test. The fly is always attached with a Duncan loop knot so it can swing freely.

On his first cast Nix deposits a Bendback Frog, one of his own creations, in a minuscule pocket well back in the pads. He first tied this deer-hair pattern in 1980, while fishing Lake O' the Pines with his son. They'd been working the pads using poppers with mono weedguards — a style better than no guard at all, but not much. One night, disgusted, Nix returned to their room at Willow Point and rummaged through his fly-tying kit, determined to make a hair popper that would pull cleanly through the snags.

In saltwater turtlegrass he'd successfully fished the Bendback streamers developed by Florida tier Chico Fernandez. The hooks of these were bent slightly at the midpoint of the shank; the wing materials were tied on to cover the point, so the fly would ride in the water with the hook turned up. Setting to work with pliers and vise, Nix adapted the same principle to freshwater surface fishing. His completed product, with splayed hackles for legs and doll eyes for extra flotation, would kick through pads and matted coontail as if it were hookless. Even so, it would set securely in the bony maw of a largemouth.

"You just throw it out there," he explains now, "and let it sit as long as you can stand it. Then give it a few pops."

The pops, once commenced, come two or three seconds apart, solid *glubs* to set a bass's nerves on edge. A fish rolls and takes but the fly burps out of its mouth, Nix's line flowing loose to the rear. He hauls on the forward stroke to pick up speed, then drops the fly dead-center on the fading swirl. But this time the bass won't have it.

The bug flicks smoothly to a succession of targets: slender channels winding through the pads, odd-shaped openings, ovals, keyholes, question marks, here and there an ancient fluted stump. In fly-fishing magazines and books, certain authorities have sought to lay down the law on casting for bass. Throw a narrow loop, they insist, to maximize velocity. Nix generally prefers wider loops, however, so the fly is delivered softly with less chance of spooking the fish. On most casts, his loops are about 2 or 3 feet wide.

The bug settles to the surface without a ripple. No action for several minutes, so Nix switches to his Bendback Snake. This pattern measures a full 6 inches long, with a reticulated head spun from deer hair in two different combinations: either black and brown, or black and olive. The long saddle hackles forming the body of the snake flare apart when dry, but cling when the fly is slipped steadily across the surface. A steady retrieve can't be achieved by stripping line (after each strip you have to let go of the line, then regrasp it), so Nix uses a hand-twist technique instead. Also, he works his rod tip gently up and down, causing the snake to undulate like a live one as it moves along.

Nearly dark; still no more strikes. Nix ties on a Dahlberg Diver — a fly he didn't originate, but has modified for his own purposes. He ties the deer-hair head broader and flatter than Dahlberg's basic design (p. 38), so the fly will dive steeper and make slightly less disturbance on the surface. Nix's retrieve is fast and vigorous: short, quick strips that make the fly plunge in a stream of bubbles, then allow it to pop back to the top.

A small bass hits, is hooked, and attempts to bore its way underneath the pads. Nix releases it and cranks up the motor, anxious to run back through the stumps while there's still some light.

In the morning Nix adopts a new plan. Only a few bass, it seems, have moved into the pads; he suspects that most are still holed up in the old channels, where the water runs 10 or 12 feet deep. He hopes to locate some takers near the surface along the edges of the channels, before the midday brightness drives them deeper. He runs up the lake to a channel that makes a horseshoe bend through coontail matted on the surface. His idea is to slip along the middle of the channel with the electric, making fairly long casts to the wall of coontail on the outside edge of the bend.

Only a few minutes into it, a fish takes a swipe at my frog but misses. Addled, I try to set the hook anyway. Nix advises casting the bug back to the same spot and letting it sit there for 6 or 8 minutes, motionless. As it happens, the wait isn't that long: a minute slips by, maybe two, and the fly simply disappears beneath the surface, no splash. This time the hook makes contact, and a good bass throws itself thrashing out of the water.

The sun is up now, barely. Scraps of cloud hang in a hazy sky, left from a storm the night before. A breeze plays across the lake, scattering light. Nix is coolly euphoric. If the conditions hold, the bass might hit along the channel edge all morning.

He fishes a Babydoll Muddler, the only bass pattern besides the diver that he uses regularly but didn't design. It was originated by his friend Robert McCurdy of Austin; it's a floating adaptation of the popular muddler streamer, with an enlarged deer-hair head and doll eyes for buoyancy. There's a soft wing of marabou, saddle hackles, and Krystal Flash. When bass want a fly that stays put on the water — when they're off their feed and couldn't care less about a fleeing tidbit — the Babydoll is Nix's choice. As long as there's a ripple on the water, the fly has plenty of action even when not retrieved. At rest it tips downward sharply at the rear, so the hook shank drops away from the wing and the marabou can squirm. The fly looks like it's treading water, as Nix says.

He holds the boat in mid-channel, nudging the electric-motor switch on and off with his bare foot. He fishes without shoes nearly all the time, so he can feel loose line on the deck and avoid stepping on it when shooting out a cast. His Babydoll alights now within an inch of the coontail; its

A 5-pounder that fell for a Shineabou Shad

googly eyes look vacantly across the water for a long minute, and then they're gone. Another nice bass, which Nix adroitly strips in and releases.

After several more hits he spots a small bunch of shad breaking the surface farther along the channel; then another, much closer. He picks through his tackle for a Shineabou Shad, a sinking pattern, then quickly works out line with a pair of false casts. By now the shad are down, but the fly settles neatly just beyond the spot where they broke. Nix lets it sink a little, then zips it along by stripping line — a retrieve he describes as "running scared." No response: and none on follow-up casts fanned out to both sides of the spot.

The clouds thicken, shuttling across the sun. Nix works the channel edge again, fishing slow, the strips short and easy, his usual way of retrieving the shad pattern when no bait is breaking. The tapered deer-hair head of the fly, and the mallard breast feathers in its wing, give it a realistic shape. Nix ties it in various lengths, 1½ to 3 inches, to duplicate the growth of shad from spring to fall.

In the middle of the channel, maybe 75 feet from the boat, the shad reappear. It's a long way but Nix leaves the electric alone, just hauls line and fires the fly out there where the surface is shaking. Then two or three strips and a 5-pound largemouth blows out of the channel, the Shineabou bright in its jaw like a pennant.

STRIP line rapidly with your rod tip high, so a freshly hooked bass can't dive into weeds. Play the fish out in the open water beside the boat.

A while later, Nix sets the boat up for a slow drift with the breeze along another weedline — more coontail matted on the surface, hanging on the brink of a deep hole. Nothing happens on the Shineabou, so Nix goes back to the Babydoll, letting it ride and writhe along the drop.

Downwind a hundred feet the weedline curves, forming a cul-de-sac where drifting plankton might collect and shad come to feed on it. Nix has been eyeing this spot and now makes out a miniature wake here and there moving against the ripples. He snaps the Babydoll off the water and gets it going in the right direction. For these extra-long shots he tightens his loops: the line knifes through the thick air and the fat, air-resistant fly turns over crisply on the final delivery. I do likewise, or try to.

When fished over schooling bait, the Babydoll produces best with a fast, noisy retrieve, a string of sharp tugs: *pop-pop-pop-pop*. From somewhere below, propelling itself upward through a glassworks of shad, a bass homes in on these persistent detonations and whacks the source right on the snoot. It's a typical school fish, perhaps a pound and a half. And there are plenty more where that one came from.

Nix pursues school bass the remainder of the morning; for this fast-break style of angling, dis-

tance casting is the norm. When feeders break the surface, casting a country mile will reach them quicker and with less disturbance than dragging the boat closer with the electric. And for casting blind — covering open water with no surface activity — long casts and the resulting long retrieves work far more efficiently than short ones, since the fly spends more time in the water, less in the air. Some experts claim long casts mean poor accuracy, plus difficulty working the fly and setting the hook; but Nix seems to have no problem at all.

Most anglers who fly-fish for bass fail to learn a productive variety of techniques. Not only do they limit themselves to short casts; they stick with fishing on the surface. Nix's great strong point is his versatility. Among other things, he's taught himself how to handle flies at different depths — to get them down wherever the bass might be at a given moment.

Nix fly-fishes for bass through most of the year, so there are times when he has to fish deep. Shallow-water fishing is good from April through late June, then the bass move deeper. But they feed in the shallows at night and will hit big, bushy topwater patterns. In cloudy weather, shallow-water fishing may also be good in morning and evening. The bass move back into the shallows in late September. Nix's favorite fishing time, October through

How Nix Retrieves at Steady Speed with the Hand Twist

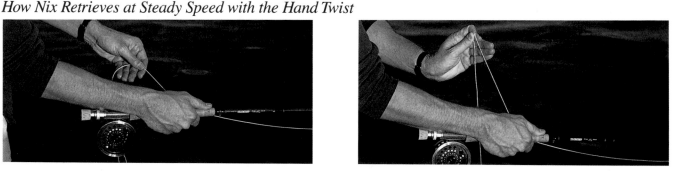

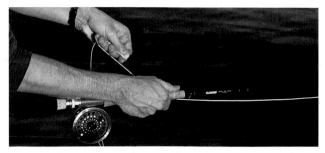

1. GRASP the line with the thumb and forefinger of the line hand. Also, keep it pinched lightly against the rod grip with the forefinger of the rod hand.

2. BEND the wrist upward and rearward to start the line and fly moving toward you. The line should meet the first joint of your little finger.

3. CATCH the line with the little-finger joint as you bend the wrist downward. A loop of line forms in your hand; the line and fly are retrieved steadily.

4. GRASP the line again, then let the loop drop from your hand. Continue gathering line in this fashion to retrieve the fly.

Flies that fool trophy bass: All these patterns are Nix's original designs, except the Dahlberg and Babydoll

Bendback Frog

Bendback Snake

Dahlberg Diver

Babydoll Muddler

Shineabou Shad

Shineabou Shiner

Fuzzabou

Fuzzy Bunny

early November, offers good topwater action. But by mid-November the bass go deep again and they stay deep until mid-February — too deep for effective fly fishing. Starting in late February and continuing through March, Nix catches some bass on sinking flies fished near bottom with a slow retrieve, but fishing is slow until the water starts to warm again in April.

The Shineabou Shad is only one of several innovative patterns Nix has developed for subsurface fishing. His Shineabou Shiner, with a tapered deer-hair head and a long wing of five different materials, is another work of realism, uncannily lifelike in shape, color, and action — his "favorite and most useful fly." He fishes it close to cover — stumps, logs, lotus pads, coontail — where shiners typically hang out. A slow retrieve usually scores best. The hand-twist technique keeps the fly swimming along smoothly, and he pauses often so the wing materials separate and flutter. If the fish are active he may use a quicker retrieve, stripping line so the fly darts forward 6 to 8 inches at a time.

For faster sinking, Nix ties special versions of the Shad and Shiner. The standard types sink very slowly because of the buoyant hair head, and are best for fishing only a foot or two deep. For depths of 3 to 8 feet, he winds lead wire on the hook shank under the body material; for getting as far down as 15 feet he forms the head of gray wool instead of deer hair, and substitutes lead eyes for the usual glass ones.

The way he ties the fly is only part of the formula; the depth reached also depends on the type of fly line. He uses three different kinds: a floating bug taper; a Teeny nymph line, which floats but has a 5-foot sinking tip; and a Scientific Anglers Constant Sink line, a full sinking type. He may start with a floating line at daybreak and stick with it a couple of hours, then switch to the Teeny and finally to the sinking line, following the fish down-

ward as the sunlight increases. He considers 15 feet the maximum practical depth: "Anything deeper than that, you need a spinning rod in your hand."

Two other sinking flies Nix has designed may simulate waterdogs or salamanders — or almost anything at all. Both have wool heads and lead eyes, and are tied in various drab shades. The Fuzzabou has a wing of marabou and Krystal Flash; the Fuzzy Bunny has a long strip of rabbit fur. He retrieves both patterns with a hand twist, occasionally raising his rod tip about 8 inches. When the fly is fished this way, the heavy lead eyes give it a jigging action.

Yet another homemade salamander imitation accounted for Nix's biggest bass. The fly is a variation of the Whitlock Hare Water Pup, with live-rubber legs on the front. "I was fishing Lake Fork Reservoir for big bass during pre-spawn when I spooked a huge fish out of the shallows. I figured it was a big bass, so I came back to the exact spot the next day. She hit on the first cast. When I set the hook, she went crazy — made half a dozen strong runs before I could grab her by the lower lip. She weighed 10-2 on my Chatillon scale."

Even though the bass would have ranked among the largest ever caught on a fly rod, Nix made the decision to release it. "Couldn't bring myself to kill her," he explained. "I'm aiming for the world fly-rod record, 13-9."

Nix never resorts to tackle other than fly equipment. He won't even carry a spinning or baitcasting rod in his boat. If the day comes when he finally pulls the new record aboard, he wants no question about the kind of tackle it was caught on.

"I stick to fly fishing," he adds, "because I've done it all my life and it's what I really know. I don't have anything against other kinds of fishing. I just like to fly-fish best."

Canoe-Country Smallmouths

by Dick Sternberg

John Herrick has probably caught more 5- to 7-pound smallmouth bass than anybody; here's how he does it

It's a long way from the Chicago Art Institute to the Quetico Provincial Park in Ontario, in terms of both miles and life style. John Herrick has spent a good deal of time in both places, and greatly prefers the latter.

He graduated from the institute in 1968 with a Bachelor of Fine Arts degree. But the mold for his life style had been cast many years earlier, when, as a twelve-year-old, he vacationed in the Quetico with his older brother. He fell in love immediately with the vast, lake-studded wilderness, and the Quetico vacation became an annual event.

When he was eighteen, the lure of the Quetico drew Herrick to a summer job guiding canoe trips.

Gradually, he learned more and more about the wilderness lakes and their fish. He learned how to catch walleyes, northern pike, and lake trout, but the species that fascinated him most was the smallmouth bass.

Several years after graduating, Herrick decided to trade the life of an artist for that of a wilderness fishing guide. So he moved to Ely, Minnesota, the gateway to the Boundary Waters Canoe Area Wilderness in northeastern Minnesota, adjacent to the Quetico. There he guided fishermen on day trips, and eventually started the canoe-outfitting and guiding business that he owns and operates today with his wife, Dina.

John Herrick

Home: *Ely, Minnesota*

Occupation: *Owner of the Moose Bay Company, a canoe-outfitting and guiding business located near the Minnesota-Ontario border*

Despite his modest, soft-spoken manner, John Herrick has gained a reputation as the premier wilderness fishing guide in the Quetico Provincial Park. His fish-catching talents have resulted in appearances on TV fishing shows, and in magazine articles describing his effective techniques. He served as a consultant to The Hunting and Fishing Library on its book, Smallmouth Bass. *If customer satisfaction is a measure of performance, John is a huge success. Most of his clients return year after year.*

Although John is an accomplished multi-species fisherman, he specializes in trophy smallmouth bass. He takes his customers to hard-to-reach, canoe-only waters where there's an excellent chance of hooking a 5- to 7-pounder. Actually, 5-pounders are quite common; in 1987, John and his customers took 25 topping the 5-pound mark. Smallmouths of 6 pounds and up are unheard of in most smallmouth waters, but over the

years John and his customers have taken more than 100 of them. His biggest went 7 pounds 6 ounces.

Getting into that trophy-smallmouth country isn't easy. You've got to go a long way back into the bush to find water where the fishing pressure is light enough for bass to get that big. John tailors his fishing trips to suit the clients' wishes and capabilities. If you're in good condition and intent on hooking a real trophy, he may take you into Crooked Lake on the Minnesota-Ontario border. The trip into Crooked requires five portages and takes almost a full day. Or he can take you to fishing almost as good on the Canadian side of Basswood Lake, which is only a four-hour canoe trip with no portages.

To preserve the quality of the smallmouth fishing, John encourages his clients to practice catch-and-release. There are plenty of walleyes and northerns for the frying pan. John kills only those smallmouths that his customers want to have mounted.

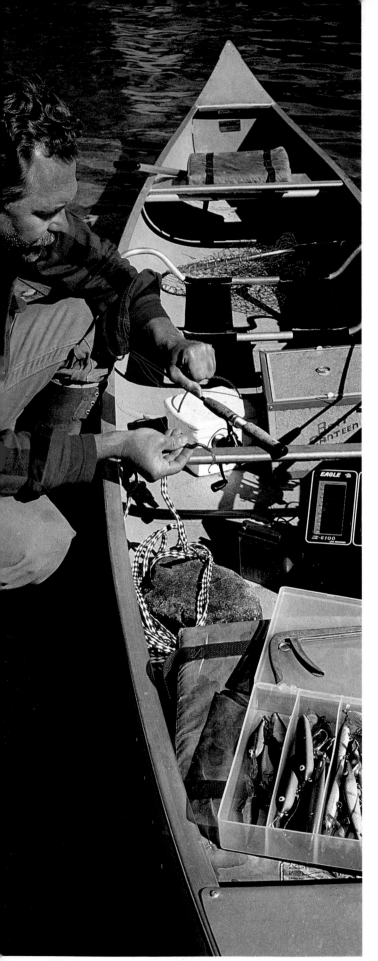

At first glance, Dina seems out of place because she more closely resembles a New York fashion model than a wilderness camp operator. Before marrying John, she worked as an ad executive in Chicago. But like him, she loves the wilderness life and wouldn't think of trading it for the city routine.

Herrick's artistic bent is obvious even on the water. He takes time out from fishing to admire a sunset and imagine what it would look like on canvas. He marvels at the sight of an osprey dive-bombing a fish, or a moose swimming across a lake. To him, the beauty of the country where he works is just as important as catching fish.

John employs several other guides at his lodge on Moose Lake, all accomplished anglers. They're constantly on the lookout for untapped smallmouth water. Within paddling distance of the lodge are tens of thousands of acres of smallmouth haunts, so the possibilities are almost endless. Sometimes John or one of the other guides will portage into some tiny, unnamed lake near one of the big lakes to check the fishing action. Over the years they have found dozens of small lakes teeming not only with smallmouths but with largemouths, walleyes, pike, and lakers. With all these potential fishing grounds, John can always catch fish somewhere.

After years of studying smallmouths and observing their seasonal movements, John knows precisely where to find them at different times of year. And he's developed techniques to suit the seasons — mainly for spring and summer, because business slacks off considerably after Labor Day.

JON BOATS with canoe racks are used for shuttling canoes to the edge of the motorless zone. Then the gear is transferred to the canoe, and you start paddling.

Herrick checks his equipment before heading out

"Smallmouth springtime activity is all centered on spawning," John observes. "In May, before they spawn, you can find them in shallow, mud-bottomed bays. Insects hatch earlier in these bays because the water is warmer, and smallmouths love to feed on the emerging larvae. I like to fish a shoreline with a southern exposure, where the sun warms the water most. You can find smallmouths almost anywhere along shore, but they concentrate around points or areas with an extended lip. Fallen trees and brush in the water also seem to concentrate them.

"For pre-spawn smallmouths, I use what I call the wait-and-wait technique. Cast a small propbait close to shore, then count to ten before moving it. Give it a subtle twitch, then wait again. Don't jerk the lure too hard — if it makes a lot of noise, it could spook the fish. When it's moved more than 5 feet from shore, forget it: you won't get a strike. Reel in and cast again.

"Another good pre-spawn lure is a floating Rapala. I use a size 11 silver. Cast to shore and retrieve with sharp twitches so the lure stays on the surface. The trick is to get the lure to change direction when you twitch — hard right to hard left.

"Big smallmouths will normally slam a surface lure, making a boil 2 feet wide. But sometimes they just peck at it, so you've got to watch carefully for any hint of a strike.

"Once they start to spawn, all they'll do is bump your lure out of the way. Then you have to go to a jig or maybe a spinner. Smallmouths may spawn almost anywhere in the lake. I find most of them

Springtime Smallmouth Habitat

ROCKY POINTS with a shallow extended lip attract smallmouths in spring. If there is deep water nearby, the fish will remain through the summer.

FALLEN TREES and submerged brush provide shallow-water cover for smallmouths. Some fish will be scattered along shore, but most will be around woody cover.

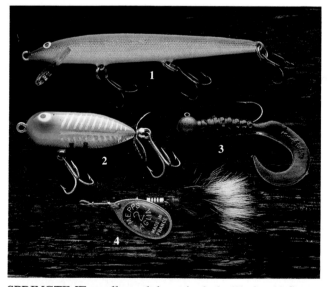

SPRINGTIME smallmouth lures include (1) size 11 floating Rapala, (2) Tiny Torpedo, (3) ¼-ounce twister-tail jig, (4) size 2 Mepps Aglia spinner.

SHELVES extending from shore draw more smallmouths than shorelines that drop off rapidly. The best shelves have plenty of boulders for cover.

CAST a Tiny Torpedo or other small propbait into openings in the brush, then wait for at least ten seconds while the ripples subside. At times, Herrick waits considerably longer, up to a full minute.

TWITCH the lure with a gentle snap of the wrists, then wait again. Make sure the lure does not disturb the surface too much or make too much noise.

WATCH for a boil that indicates a strike, then set the hook. Sometimes the strike may not be as obvious — all you will see is a small ring when the fish nips at the lure.

along a shoreline with a southern or southwestern exposure and small pea- to fist-sized gravel; usually they're next to a boulder or log. But they may also spawn on big, shallow reefs.

"For spawners, it's tough to beat a black or unpainted jig head with a smoke twister tail. I use a ⅛- or ¼-ounce head, depending on the water depth. I've experimented with colors, and others will work; but this combination is the most consistent. Another dependable lure is a number 2 or 3 Mepps with a silver blade and squirrel-tail dressing. Live bait works well, too. My favorite is a leech or nightcrawler on a size 6 hook, with only a split-shot for weight. Drop it anywhere near their nest and they'll grab it.

"After spawning, fishing for big smallmouths can be tough. Most of the trophy fish are females, and they stop feeding for a couple of weeks when spawning is completed. The males will bite as long as they're guarding the nest; but when the fry leave, males may be tough to catch too. Post-spawn smallmouths want easy food, like insect larvae. You can use the same lures and baits you used earlier, but you've got to move them real slow.

"In the springtime, fishing is best in the afternoon. I tell my clients to relax and have a good breakfast — there's no need to get on the water at the crack of dawn. Actually, afternoon fishing tends to be best all year. I can't explain it, but this seems to hold true.

"Early-summer fishing can be a little trickier than spring fishing," John continues, "because the smallmouths may be shallow or deep. I've even seen them suspended over deep water, feeding on ciscoes. If they're done spawning and I'm not really sure what depth they're at, I use the high-low system.

"The high-low system is like a broad-spectrum antibiotic. While my customer pitches propbaits or floating Rapalas into the shallows, I paddle the canoe and fish a jig over the side in the deep water. We soon find the best depth. But sometimes we both catch fish, at different depths.

"By midsummer, most of the smallmouths go deep. This is the time when fishing is most dependable. You know where they are — you just need to find out what they're hitting. Jigs still take some fish, but live bait is the consistent producer. I prefer leeches and nightcrawlers. I'm sure live minnows would work too, but it's illegal to bring them into Canada. Funny thing: smallmouths are usually stuffed with crayfish, but when I've tried live crayfish I haven't had much luck.

"One of the problems on a summertime canoe trip is keeping your bait alive. If it dies, you've got a long haul back to the nearest bait shop.

Working the shoreline at sunset — Basswood Lake

Crawlers keep well in damp moss

"Leeches keep pretty well in a styrofoam bucket if you change the water often and keep them out of the sun. Crawlers are tough to keep in hot weather. But if you put them in a Bait Canteen and soak the fiberboard sides, evaporation will keep them cool.

"The key to locating summertime smallmouths is finding a spot with a sandy bottom and sparse weed growth. The lakes I fish are on the Precambrian Shield, and their basins are mostly rock. A sandy, weedy bottom produces more food, so that's where a lot of the big smallmouths hang out.

"My favorite midsummer spots are big reefs topping off at 10 feet or less. The best ones have a combination of sand, rocks, and cabbage weed on them, and water at least 40 feet deep within 50 yards. But any spot with the right bottom type and with deep water nearby may hold smallmouths. It might be a main-lake point, a dropoff adjacent to an island, or just a shoreline break. It's not unusual to find walleyes on the same structure, only about 5 feet deeper.

"When searching for smallmouths, I use a technique very similar to backtrolling with an outboard. I point the stern of the canoe into the wind, then scull backward with one hand. An LCR powered by a motorcycle battery helps me follow the contour. Normally, I use a ¼-ounce slip-sinker rig baited with a leech or crawler.

"A few years back, I stumbled onto a terrific live-bait method ideal for fishing a reef or point from a canoe. It's called the swing technique. The man I was guiding brought his wife along, but she wasn't too interested in fishing. I set both of them up with a leech on a split-shot rig, then anchored the canoe so it swung back and forth over a reef. He and I started casting and retrieving; she just dropped her rig over the side, reeled up a turn or two from the bottom, laid her rod across the canoe, and began reading a book. Wouldn't you know it — she was

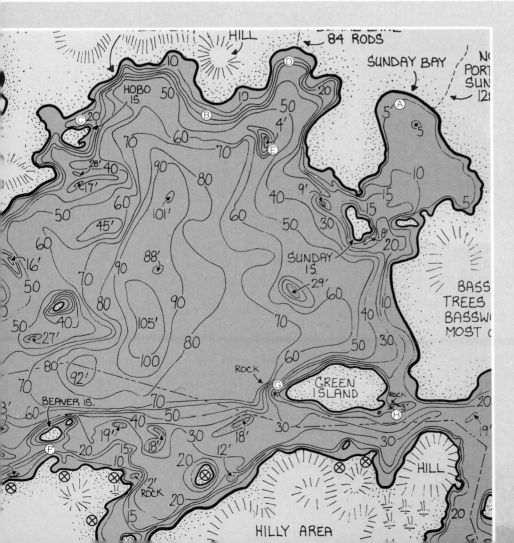

Where Herrick Finds Smallmouths in Shield Lakes

In spring through early summer, smallmouths can be found near their spawning areas which include: (A) shallow bays; (B) extended shoreline lips; and (C) narrows just outside shallow bays; all these have southern exposures, sand-gravel bottoms, and scattered boulders or logs for spawning cover. After spawning, the fish begin moving to their summer locations which include: (D) cabbage beds along sandy shoreline breaks adjacent to deep water; (E) sunken islands adjacent to deep water that top off at 10 feet or less, with a bottom of sand, rocks, and cabbage; (F) channels between islands and shoreline; (G) major points, either on islands or the main-lake shoreline; and (H) sandbars with scattered rock and sandgrass extending from islands or the main-lake shoreline. Smallmouth remain in their summer locations well into August. (NOTE: This map is intended to show the types of spots Herrick recommends, not the actual spots he fishes.)

catching practically all the fish. Finally we did the same, and our success really picked up.

"The technique is a lot like slip-bobber fishing because the bait dangles in front of the fish, tantalizing them into striking. But it works even better because the canoe swings slowly from side to side, covering more area than you can with a slip-bobber. You might say it's a no-brainer method, but it really works."

A fishing trip with John Herrick is an experience you won't soon forget. For those who live in a big city, the atmosphere of the Boundary Waters is surely a welcome relief. Instead of police sirens at night, you hear wolves howling. There's no whining of outboard motors; in fact, you may never see another canoe. And the smallmouth fishing could safely be called the best in the world. You might find slightly bigger smallmouths in a few southern reservoirs, but for numbers of trophy-class fish, John's area is unparalleled.

There's only one problem: John is an exceptional camp cook. So if you thought paddling the canoe would help trim a few pounds ... well, forget it.

How to "Backtroll" with a Canoe

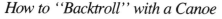

POINT the stern of the canoe into the wind, then push the paddle toward the bow with a powerful stroke.

TURN the paddle sideways after the stroke to reduce water resistance; reposition for another stroke.

The Swing Technique

LOWER a rock off the stern of the canoe to anchor well upwind of the reef you intend to fish.

PAY OUT rope until the canoe is over the tip of the reef. Lower your line to bottom, then reel up a foot or two. The wind will swing the canoe and your line across the reef. Pay out more rope to cover more of the reef.

Buggin' Bronzebacks

by Nat Franklin Jr.

Stream smallmouth can't resist the bass bugs created by Larry Dahlberg

Picture a young boy during a drowsy 1950s summer, in a village in the pulpwood country of northwestern Wisconsin. On this particular afternoon he dawdles on his way home from Bible school, his mind inflamed as usual with fishing. He halts atop the dam of a public pond called Memory Lake — a romantic label at variance with the silt-clogged reality — and from this vantage spots numerous porker carp wallowing in the shallows below.

For a moment, he mulls the probable consequences of what he has in mind. Then, in a flash, he's up to his waist in Memory Lake, thrashing the sour water so the carp come bumping into him in a frenzy of mistaken identity. One by one he drags them buckling from the pond, their scales as big and shiny as half dollars. When the water flattens out, twenty fat carp lie gasping on the grassy bank. Out of breath himself, the boy delivers the whole mess to

---

Larry Dahlberg

Home: *Brainerd, Minnesota*

Occupation: *Producer-director of the* In-Fisherman *television series*

Larry Dahlberg is well known among fly fishermen as the creator of the Dahlberg Diver, the most important new fly design in several decades for bass and other warm-water fish. Though the fly was not introduced to anglers until 1983, when an article about it appeared in Fly Fisherman *magazine, he first tied and fished it in the mid-1960s, while still a teenager. Dahlberg also introduced the revolutionary material called Flashabou, which resembles narrow metallic tinsel but is far more flexible, for use in fly wings, jig tails, and other lure dressings.*

He started fishing at age four with his father, tossing Dardevles on 50-pound-test line into a small pond in Grantsburg, Wisconsin. His father was a stickler for casting accuracy, setting a box under a swing set as a target and having him practice long hours. Dahlberg's first fly rod was an ice-fishing pole 4½ feet long that his father rigged for him with a weight-forward line —

a tough rig to cast under the swings with, but he persevered and in time became expert.

Dahlberg may have set a record for youthfulness in the guiding profession: he began work as a smallmouth bass guide on the St. Croix River near his home when he was only eleven. A fly-fishing club on the river needed someone who knew the river and could row a boat. "I'd only fished for smallmouths incidentally," he says, "catching a few while out for muskies. And I'd fly-fished only for sunfish with my 4½-footer." But he had the knack, and wound up guiding 23 summers; in time, he also started managing the club facilities for the wealthy owners.

Since 1986 Dahlberg has been the producer-director of the popular In-Fisherman *television series. He appears in many of the episodes himself, fishing across North America and elsewhere, often with a fly rod. He thinks the series is an excellent vehicle for introducing anglers to fly fishing. "The biggest fly-fishing magazine has maybe a 140,000 circulation; the show has more than 20 million viewers. So we may have exposed more people to fly fishing than all the magazines and books ever written on it."*

a family of grateful Hungarian immigrants who live nearby.

Such benevolence cuts no ice when he arrives back home. His mother surveys his carp-slimed Bible-school clothes and orders him to the backyard, there to give them a prompt and decent burial. The clothes won't be alone out there. It isn't the first time all this has happened.

Larry Dahlberg, the hero of this drama, is not and never has been a purist of any sort. He's famous today as an expert fly fisherman — a reputation which could easily give some people the wrong idea. But the angler who noodled for carp and buried his trousers is not about to limit himself to fly tackle, nor to trout or any other single species of fish. Most of the time, in fact, he fishes with spinning or baitcasting gear. And the range of fish he pursues — with flies and otherwise — includes everything from bass and trout to muskies and tarpon.

But it's true, certainly, that fly fishing is his favorite method. And the fish he'd far rather catch than any other is the smallmouth bass. "It's the first in my heart," he says, "maybe because I guided fly fishermen for smallmouths for so long."

As he speaks, he stands thigh-deep in the St. Croix River, the stream on the Wisconsin-Minnesota border where he did all that guiding. It's now late summer, and the water is low and clear. To avoid spooking

fish, he's waded quietly into position about 60 feet from a stony, brush-covered point extending into the stream. The point is undercut, and the intervening water is fast and broken, with a bottom of rocks the size and color of bread loaves. Smallmouths might be almost anywhere. The prime spot, surely, is the undercut itself — but the irregular bottom away from the bank could also hold resting or feeding fish.

After casting very close to the point, Dahlberg begins retrieving with a series of short strips. His fly is a Dahlberg Diver, chartreuse. With each quick

Dahlberg Diver

strip of line, it darts slightly under the surface; then, immediately, it floats back up in the brief pause before the next strip begins. Dahlberg holds

Dahlberg fishes his Diver past an undercut point on Wisconsin's St. Croix River

his rod tip high, at nearly a 45-degree angle from the water, giving it a little flip every time he strips, to make the fly dart more vigorously. When the fly has moved out 6 or 7 feet from the point, he retrieves with longer, faster skips that pull it a foot or so under the water and keep it at about that level, darting forward.

On his second cast to the same spot, a smallmouth hits beside the undercut and he plays it for a couple of minutes in the swift current — a 2-pounder. He explains how he settled on his tactics. The diver was an ideal choice for this spot, he says, since it could make some disturbance at the surface on the first part of the retrieve, attracting any fish tucked up under the point; then, as it worked farther out, he could plunge it deeper for fish holding on the rocky bottom of the run.

Divers are the only flies that you can fish on the surface and well beneath it on the same cast. They're unsurpassed for any fishing situation where such a double-feature retrieve is called for. You can work a diver through shallow water or over weeds or deadfalls, then pull it down under when deeper or more open water is reached. Dahlberg got the inspiration for his diver when fishing with spinning and baitcasting plugs that float at rest but dive when retrieved. "I wanted to make a fly with an up-and-down diving action, something like a Suick [a muskie jerkbait]."

Not surprisingly, the Dahlberg Diver bears some resemblance to a plug. The head is large and rounded, made of trimmed deer hair, with a collar of untrimmed hair at its upper back edge; the whole thing is shaped like a badminton shuttlecock. When the fly is pulled sharply, water flows over the head and hits the collar, pushing it underwater. Dahlberg's innovation, originally intended for bass, has now been used to catch everything from trophy rainbows to tarpon to innumerable weird-named fish on faraway continents.

Dahlberg ties his diver in a number of different ways. One variation has a wing of marabou and saddle hackles, with a few strands of Flashabou for extra attraction. This works well for smallmouths, but he considers a rabbit-strip diver even better. It has a long, narrow tail made from a strip of rabbit fur still attached to the tanned hide. For smallmouths he generally ties the diver in white, yellow, chartreuse, or a natural rabbit gray. When he fishes it fast, he prefers the brighter attractor colors; slow, the natural gray.

The best diver sizes for smallmouths, Dahlberg says, are 1 and 1/0. To help keep the diver from soaking up water (this is true of his other hair bugs

as well), he applies a paste floatant sparingly to the head before fishing.

For nearly all his smallmouth fishing, with the diver or any other fly, Dahlberg uses a 7-weight, 8-foot 9-inch Sage RP graphite rod. He prefers a standard weight-forward line to a bug taper; he feels that the standard type forms a smoother casting loop and reaches longer distances when necessary. His leaders are 9½-footers with 8- to 12-pound tippets. All the lines he uses for smallmouths are floaters.

When he wants to get deep in current, he simply attaches a split-shot a foot up the leader from the fly, then another shot 8 inches farther up. He points out that a floating line can be picked up off the water for a new cast far more easily than a sink-tip line, a type he avoids altogether. The split-shot are easy enough to cast, he says. The trick is to keep your line speed fast, so the shot-loaded leader won't sag in the air and foul on the fly line.

Later, a different stretch of the St. Croix: the water is flat here, a long pool that extends out of sight both upstream and down but has a visible current around deadfalls along both banks. Dahlberg faces shore from a casting position on the bow deck of his 13-foot Boston Whaler. Though short, the boat is broad and stable. The casting deck is a slab of marine plywood he installed himself, affixing it atop the gunwales for maximum casting height and visibility.

Dahlberg battles a smallmouth from his casting deck

Mounted on this forward deck is a powerful 24-volt electric motor. The outboard is a 40-horse whose speed enables him to fish stretches of the river that lie far from any bridge, and to do so in a single day's fishing rather than making a two- or three-day expedition. The shallow-draft hull floats in only 2 or 3 inches of water, so he can slip down through the thinnest riffles by tilting the outboard up and maneuvering with a 12-foot graphite push pole of the type used for saltwater flats fishing.

Back under the deadfalls, big smallmouths lie in ambush. But getting them out is no cinch. Where the trunks and limbs rest directly on the water, Dahlberg shoots out a cast parallel to them but several feet upstream. For this, he typically uses a hair popper, letting it drift motionless on the surface until it moves within a foot or two of the obstruction. Then he brings it in at medium speed, with short strips so the bug makes a series of light popping sounds. He calls this his "buzzbait retrieve." His cast goes just far enough back along the obstruction — and then his retrieve is just fast enough — that he can pull the bug into open water before it drifts onto the snag and hangs up. These tactics work best in water 4 feet deep or less, Dahlberg says.

Where leaning trees and brush have not quite collapsed onto the water but still hang just above it, he casts back under as far as possible. The trick here — and Dahlberg is a master — is to side-cast low,

sometimes within inches of the water, keeping the line moving rapidly so the tip and fly don't sag to the surface and spoil the presentation. The keys to line speed are the double haul and extremely narrow casting loops — only a foot wide at most. "In fly fishing for smallmouths," Dahlberg says, "a narrow loop is *always* best." He's able to flick a bug all the way back to the bank, even where a tree hangs down near the water some 50 feet out in the stream.

Once he's got a bug adrift under the cover, he may work it back out with the steady popping retrieve already described. Or he may substitute a retrieve that simulates a swimming frog — allowing the popper to rest briefly, then popping it two or three times in quick succession, following this with another rest, and so on. With either type of retrieve, he advises sliding the bug about 3 feet across the surface just before lifting it off for another cast. "If they're looking at it, they may show themselves when you do this and you'll know where they are. Then you cast right back to the same place on your next shot."

Yet another productive retrieve with the popper is simply to let it sit motionless while it floats past logs. This works especially well, Dahlberg says, when the smallmouths are spooky in low, clear water. The one thing to avoid is exactly the sort of retrieve that most bass fly-rodders generally use: giving the bug one big pop and letting it sit awhile,

Deadfalls in current: prime spot for Dahlberg's "buzzbait retrieve" with his hair popper

then uncorking another big pop — the same tedious procedure over and over. "That's the least productive retrieve there is, in all my experience," he says.

One more important point that Dahlberg emphasizes in fishing poppers for smallmouths: always fish upstream or across stream. If you try to retrieve a popper against the current, it will dig into the water and make an enormous fish-spooking boil — not to mention that the popper will be almost impossible to pick off the water for another cast.

Dahlberg Slider

Hair popper tied by Dahlberg

Dahlberg's deer-hair poppers have a flattened face, doll eyes, and saddle hackles separated to suggest the legs of a frog. He prefers hair poppers to cork or plastic types. Hair bugs cast better, because of their lighter weight, and the softness of the body seems to fool a striking bass into holding on a moment longer, giving the angler some extra reaction time for making the hook-set. Since the popper is fished relatively slow, he likes natural colors — green and light gray-brown — the latter the shade of undyed deer hair. The best sizes for smallmouth bass are 1 and 1/0.

Another great surface bug — one that few bass fly rodders are likely to have fished — is the Dahlberg Slider. This design also has a head of clipped deer hair, but it's bullet-shaped. Unlike the diver, the slider is designed to stay on the surface. And unlike a popper, it can be fished in any direction relative to the current. Even if you retrieve it straight upstream, it skims across the water with no tendency to dig in.

"Slider-type bugs were developed in the early days of fly fishing in the U.S.," Dahlberg says. "I just went from an old type called a Wilder-Dilg that had a cork head, and tied my own fly with a hair head." He uses sliders in sizes 1 and 2. White and yellow are his color choices, so he can see the fly easily on the surface.

His favorite place to fish the slider is what he calls a "current push" — a slick run of rocky water 1 to 4 feet deep, just above a riffle that acts like a dam. He casts across stream or slightly downstream, then

allows the fly to skate on the surface and swing until it's straight below him. All the while the fly is skating, he holds his rod up at a 45-degree angle, to avoid getting too much belly in the line. A small amount of belly will make the fly skate at just the right speed; a large belly will drag it too fast and may also make hook-sets difficult.

He follows the swing with his rod tip. Though a steady drift will take fish, an erratic one often is better, accomplished by bouncing the rod tip while holding it upward. If he sees the fly is going to swing short of some spot he wants to reach — a large boulder, for instance — he'll feed as much line as needed on the drift. A smallmouth may surface out of nowhere at any moment during the drift, bulging up beneath the river's gloss to slam the slider.

When the fly has swung straight below him, Dahlberg retrieves just enough line to enable a pickup for another cast. He makes four casts in one spot, then moves on downstream to the next. "It's an easy technique for beginners," he says. "And you can do it while wading, but it helps to get up high in a boat. Why do smallmouths hit this dumb-looking bug skidding along like nothing they've ever seen before? I don't know."

SKATE a slider over a "current push." After casting across stream, raise the rod as shown; a moderate belly forms in the line, skating the fly.

For smallmouths in faster water, Dahlberg's usual choice is his Flashdancer, a streamer with a deer-hair head and a wing consisting entirely of strands of Flashabou. This material squirms in the current, emitting flashes of light in every conceivable direction. It comes in a variety of metallic colors — blue, red, pearl, you name it — but gold and silver are

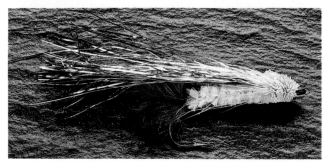

Flashdancer, an attractor pattern

by far his favorites. The Flashdancer may resemble a baitfish, but Dahlberg sees it mainly as a nonrealistic attractor pattern. He calls it his "Mepps imitation." For smallmouths he prefers sizes 1/0 to 2.

The trick to fishing an attractor, he says, is to keep it moving fast enough that the bass don't have time to study it closely. If they do, they'll see it's a fake, something to avoid. "Smallmouths are programmed through natural selection to hit anything that looks like it doesn't belong, to get rid of it. You especially want to fish an attractor fast if the water is clear. You want them to glimpse it, just get a look. Give them the impression that if they don't hit it right now, it'll get away."

Dahlberg usually casts the Flashdancer across stream, then retrieves it in short jerks as it swings with the current. The jerks are produced partly with

his line hand, partly by shaking the rod tip. He doesn't mend line, just holds the tip high to keep much of his line off the water; the minor drag caused by the remaining belly does not discourage strikes from smallmouths.

Flashabou, the main ingredient of the Flashdancer, is now sold by virtually every dealer in fly-tying materials and is used in countless other flies and lures. Its history goes back to Dahlberg's early days on the St. Croix. He was fourteen or fifteen at the time, guiding a woman who wasn't highly skilled at fly fishing. "She had to fly-fish, because her husband would bring her along to the club and that's all they did there. She had to put in a dollar bet for the biggest fish every day, a dollar for the first, a dollar for the most. She paid off gamely for years."

Then Dahlberg got the idea of tying streamers with some flexible gold Christmas-tree tinsel he'd seen; he gave all the new flies to his female client. "The tinsel was 1/32 inch wide, much wider than Flashabou is now, but it worked. She'd keep track of her bass by bending over matches in a matchbook. Before lunch, she'd have all the matches bent, and notches in the cover besides. I kept the fly just to her for a couple of years. We let all the others stew, all trying to figure out how she was doing so well."

Much later, Dahlberg trademarked the name Flashabou for a material similar to the tree tinsel. Flashabou was first sold in the late 1970s; it's now made in twenty colors and is used in flies of all types, from the tiniest trout midges to the biggest tarpon streamers.

This material was followed by another of Dahlberg's innovations, a colored synthetic fiber called

Dahlberg casts across a riffle, setting up a drift with his Flashdancer streamer

Hairabou. His idea was to make a hair especially for big flies, a material much longer than any animal hair that was readily available. The stuff also had to be wavy, so it would give the fly a bulky look with relatively few fibers: a fly tied with too much thick, wind-resistant hair would make casting difficult. A friend of Dahlberg's who was a chemist in the wig business came to his aid. Today, Hairabou has become a favorite material in extra-long flies for lunker bass, and also for pike, muskies, and saltwater fish.

Toward the end of a day on the river, as Dahlberg works along a shoreline in his Whaler, casting poppers and divers to logs crisscrossed like Oriental calligraphy, he hooks, boats, and releases dozens of smallmouths weighing up to 4½ pounds. The particular appeal of fly fishing — obvious to some anglers, obscure to others — seems absolutely clear to Dahlberg: "Fly fishing is comparatively non-mechanical. When you fight a smallmouth with fly tackle, you're not using a reel, just your hands on the line. There's no drag device between you and the fighting fish.

"When you were a little kid and you hooked a fish, you had this feeling of … who's got who? You weren't at all sure you were going to catch him. He might get off any moment. It made your heart beat faster. Fishing with a fly rod is like that, even now. You can't just roll 'em over on their side and reel 'em in. Fly fishing really is more exciting."

Dahlberg admires a 4-pound St. Croix smallmouth, which he'll quickly set free

Bass Tips

Bass Tips from Tony Bean
Trimming the Pork for Tailored Action

One of Bean's favorite smallmouth lures is what he calls a "fly and rind" — actually a ⅛- or ¼-ounce hair jig dressed with a pork chunk. The chunk is an Uncle Josh 101 or 11; both styles have the size and shape he likes. At times, Bean trims part or all of the fat from the chunk, to change the sink rate and action of his offering. When the water is cold or the smallmouths are sluggish for any other reason, he wants a slower drop and less action. When the water is warm and the fish more active, he prefers a fast-sinking lure with increased action.

TONY BEAN has caught more than 200 smallmouth bass weighing 5 pounds and up. He lives in Nashville and guides anglers for smallmouths on Percy Priest Reservoir and other southern waters. He's written a book, *Tony Bean's Smallmouth Guide*.

Offset Hook for Sure Sets

To increase his hooking percentage with jigs, Bean bends the hook so the point aims slightly to the side. This way, he says, the point takes a better bite in the side of the fish's jaw. He believes it should be bent to the left (looking at the lure head-on) for a right-handed angler, and the opposite way for a left-hander.

SLICE fat off a pork chunk to alter the sink rate and action. An untrimmed chunk (left) sinks slower and has less action than a trimmed one (right).

TURN the hook point of a jig outward with needlenose pliers, shifting it only a short distance from the original position.

44

Bobby Brewster
Soft Jigging Spoon for Deep Bass

A highly effective slow-dropping lure for large-mouths is a 1/16-ounce jig with a Gitzit or other tube-style soft-plastic dressing. One drawback of the lure is that for deep fishing — 15 feet down, or more — it takes too much time to sink. Bobby Brewster, a guide and competition angler from Elephant Butte, New Mexico, says that he and other pros who fish deep southwestern reservoirs have a solution. They combine a larger tube-style dressing with a heavy jigging spoon. The spoon has a rapid sink rate, ideal for fishing the depths, and the dressing gives the whole lure a soft texture so the bass won't spit it out before you have a chance to set the hook.

SLIP a tube-style dressing over a ¾-ounce Hopkins jigging spoon, just far enough that the eye and split-ring of the spoon protrude. The treble will be partially hidden in the legs of the dressing.

Mike Teigen
Weedless Bullet-Sinker Jig

One big problem with ordinary weedless jigs is that stems, leaves, and other bits of debris catch too easily on the hook eye where it protrudes from the head. Mike Teigen, a guide and competition angler from Osage, Minnesota, fishes for largemouths in wild rice, bulrushes, and reeds, and makes his own special weedless jigs to solve the problem. For a jig head he uses a bullet sinker that has a live-rubber skirt, such as the Culprit Captivator or the Gopher Worm Dancer. Behind this he positions a keeper worm hook, with a piece of plastic worm covering the keeper and hook point. Part of the keeper is clipped off, so it won't fill the hook gap and interfere with hooking. The piece of worm is what makes the lure so weedless; hard worms such as Creme and Culprit hold up best. Though he could attach a whole plastic worm this same way for snag protection, Tiegen prefers a pork-chunk trailer. When fishing slow in the weeds, he says the chunk will catch more bass.

Conrad Peterson
Double Trailers for Sure Hooking

At times, a buzzbait cranked across the surface at high speed will trigger bass like nothing else. The problem, though, is that they often miss the speeding lure, striking somewhere behind it. This happened to Conrad Peterson, a tackle-company owner from Aitkin, Minnesota, on a trip to Texas. The buzzer would draw bass out of flooded trees, but he couldn't connect. He decided to attach a trailer hook, but didn't stop at just one. His strung-out buzzbait — with one trailer riding point-down, and another point-up — did the trick. The rear hook extended past the skirt on the bait, getting even the shortest strikers. And Peterson noticed that many of his bass were hooked in the upper jaw, on the downturned hook. These fish apparently struck from below: he would probably have missed them if all the hooks had been turned up in the usual way.

ADD a pair of trailer hooks to increase your hooking percentage with a high-speed buzzbait or spinnerbait retrieve. The point on the front trailer rides down; on the rear trailer, up.

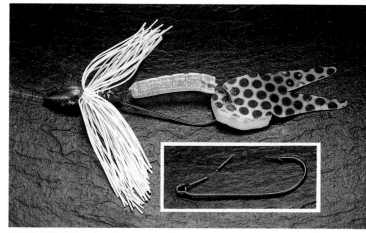

RIG a weedless bass jig by threading 20-pound mono through a skirted bullet sinker, then tying it to a 5/0 Mister Twister keeper hook. Push a section of toothpick into the sinker hole from the bottom, to peg the sinker in place against the hook eye. Attach a pork chunk to the hook. Clip part of the keeper off the hook (inset), leaving only the last two barbs. Thread a 1-inch piece of hard plastic worm onto the keeper and then onto the hook point.

Walleye & Sauger

Wheat-Country Walleyes

by Dick Sternberg

North Dakota guide Clayton Folden discloses his system for trophy walleyes, plus bonus saugers and saugeyes

Fishing guides are noted for their astounding ability to explain why the fish quit biting just before you arrived. So when I pulled into New Town, North Dakota, to fish with Clayton Folden, it was with some apprehension that I asked him, "How's fishin'?"

Clayton started his reply on the typical negative note. "Barometer's way up and the fish moved deep. The guys I had out yesterday blew a bunch of big fish." But then he continued in a matter-of-fact tone: "We wound up with a nice mess of saugers and six walleyes over 8 pounds. Biggest was just under 12." Not bad for adverse conditions and clutzy fishermen.

For Clayton Folden, days like that are the rule, not the exception. My goal on our four-day trip was to observe his fishing techniques, pick his brain, and otherwise try to determine the secrets to his consistent walleye- and sauger-fishing success.

"Before you try fishin' Sakakawea, you'd better have the right equipment," Clayton warned. "Most people aren't used to winds like we got around here. Lots of days it blows over 30 miles an hour and the big lake gets plenty rough. If I waited for calm weather, I wouldn't fish much, so I need a boat that can handle it."

Clayton Folden

Home: *New Town, North Dakota*

Occupation: *Fishing guide and manager of Van Hook Traynor Park and Recreation Area*

A burly, sandy-haired Norwegian with an easygoing, likable nature, Clayton Folden is widely regarded as

North Dakota's top fishing guide. He's also an accomplished tournament angler, routinely claiming one of the top spots in regional walleye-sauger contests.

Folden does most of his fishing on Lake Sakakawea, also known as Garrison Reservoir. This giant Missouri River impoundment sprawls halfway across North Dakota, from Garrison on the east to Williston on the west.

Folden has guided on Sakakawea since 1981 and has fished there regularly for about 20 years. He was born

near New Town and has lived in the area all his life. "No reason to move," he observes. "Got the best fishing in the world right here."

That's a pretty ambitious claim, but Folden can present some awfully strong arguments. In 1971, Lake Sakakawea produced the current world-record sauger, a monster weighing 8 pounds 12 ounces. On an average day, Folden boats two to three dozen saugers in the 2- to 4-pound class. When fishing is really hot, he may catch over a hundred.

The walleyes are fewer in number, but their size is astonishing. Folden figures he has caught at least a hundred over 10 pounds. He releases most of his big ones, so he doesn't keep precise size records.

When not guiding, Folden enjoys combing Sakakawea's shorelines and islands for Indian relics. Over the years, he's put together a magnificent collection of arrowheads, hide scrapers, and other Indian tools. He also enjoys hunting waterfowl and upland birds, which he finds in abundance out his back door.

Heading out on Sakakawea in early morning

Clayton's 17-foot Yar-Craft is ideal for the rough water. "Tried a lot of different boats," he recalled. "But the Yar-Craft has a fiberglass hull molded just the right way to throw the water sideways. I can run 3-foot waves with the boat loaded and take only a little spray. With most aluminum boats, I'd get a real bath.

"I use a sea anchor to help control the boat when I'm drifting or slow-trolling. It slows the boat speed and makes steering easier, because the wind doesn't swing the bow as much. Trolling plates also help in windy weather. A local outfit makes 'em — never

seen 'em anywhere else. The spring-loaded plates automatically drop down from the transom when you backtroll, and flip back up when you go forward. When it's really windy, I use the sea anchor together with the trolling plates to control the boat and go slow enough.

Folden's trolling plates in the down position

"I've got a pair of splash guards on the transom for backtrolling, but backtrolling only works when the water's not too rough. When it's real rough, I drift with the sea anchor out the bow, using the motor to slide in and out to follow a cut."

Clayton is an extremely versatile fisherman, employing a variety of artificial-lure and live-bait techniques. Following are descriptions of his favorite walleye- and sauger-fishing methods.

How to Use a Sea Anchor

MAKE sure the bag and straps are not tangled; clip the rope to the boat's bow eye. Drop the bag overboard.

WIND DIRECTION

DRIFT with the wind along a break, the bag slows your speed considerably. Adjust your course with the motor.

SLOW your trolling speed with the sea anchor. It works equally well for backtrolling (shown) or forward trolling.

PICK UP the bag by pulling the rope, then grabbing the narrow end of the bag (inset) to empty the water.

Walleye

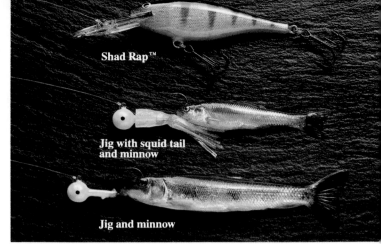

Folden's favorite walleye lures

"There's lots of ways of catchin' walleyes," Clayton noted, "but I like to get 'em on jigs. It's fun to feel that little tick when they hit. There's times when I know I could catch more on a bottom-bouncer rig [p. 52], but I fish a jig anyway. Jigs work all season, but they're best in spring and fall.

"In summer, the fish are usually scattered over big flats less than 15 feet deep, so I do a lot of trolling with size 9 Shad Raps, usually perch color. But when I find a school of fish, I switch back to jigs.

"I like a ¼-ounce chartreuse jig head with a big hook, about 3/0. Sometimes I fish a plain jig head tipped with a minnow, sometimes I put on a chartreuse squid tail and a minnow. I hook the minnow right through the bony part of its head — that way it stays on the hook a long time.

"The big jig hook's important — it'll catch a lot more walleyes than a small hook. I test the hook with my fingernail to make sure it's sharp enough — if the point slides across your nail without sticking, it needs to be sharpened.

"Most of the time, I use fatheads for tipping jigs, but sucker minnows about 4 inches long will work

too. Good bait's tough to get around here — we don't have much of a selection.

"The fish in this lake won't hesitate to take a big minnow 'cause they're used to feeding on 4- to 6-inch smelt." The smelt were stocked in the lake in 1971 and have since become extremely abundant. They provide most of the food for the walleyes and saugers and account for their extraordinary size. "I've counted fifteen big smelt in the belly of one walleye," Clayton recalled.

"For jig fishing, I like a 5½-foot, fast-action spinning outfit with 6-pound mono. I use TriMax line

'cause it's thin and tough. For trolling, I use a 5½-foot, fast-action baitcasting outfit with 8- to 10-pound TriMax.

"Sometimes I cast the jig right up to shore and retrieve it in short hops. Other times I bounce it along right below the boat. It all depends on what the fish are doin'.

"Walleyes are real unpredictable. I've seen 'em so shallow their back fins were stickin' out of the water. Next day they might be in 25 foot. But they're gonna bite somewhere every day — I don't care about moon changes, cold fronts, or nuthin'. Somebody gets 'em somewhere.

"The barometer makes a big difference in where you're gonna find 'em and how they're gonna bite. I like a steady barometer between 29.90 and 30.10. When it's higher, the walleyes go deep and don't bite as good."

I've never been much on following the barometer, but on our recent trip, Clayton's theory proved rock-solid. For the first two days, the barometer held fairly steady in the desired range. We found most of the walleyes at a depth of 5 to 10 feet, and they hit sharply on ¼-ounce jigs tipped with minnows. In the two days, we caught twenty-four walleyes over 7 pounds, including three 10s, one 11 and two 12s.

When I met Clayton on the third day, he mentioned that the barometer read 30.20 that morning and was still rising. We tried fishing shallow with no success, but found a few good-sized walleyes at 20 feet. They were hitting short, and we had to tip our jigs with smaller minnows to catch them. The barometer continued to rise through the fourth day.

The walleyes moved to 25 feet and bit even softer. Our final walleye count for the last two days was six, with the largest about 9 pounds. It may have been a coincidence, but I'll be watching the barometer more closely from now on.

Clayton pays little attention to cloud cover. "Sunny weather don't bother me a'tall," he stated flatly. "Water's kinda murky here and light penetration's pretty low. But I do like a little wind, 'specially for big walleyes.

"When the wind pounds in, it blows in food and attracts smelt and other baitfish. Then the walleyes move in to feed and you can really nail 'em by casting in to shore.

"I like to anchor and cast in. It's a lot easier than fightin' the wind with your motor, and you won't spook the walleyes. But it takes a heavy anchor and a lot of rope to hold the boat. I carry a 25-pound grapple anchor and 100 feet of rope.

"When it's calm, you may have to fish deeper," Clayton advised. To cover a wider depth range, he often uses a "meat line," which is a 10-pound line rigged with a 1- to 2-ounce Bottom Walker; a 2½-foot, 6- to 8-pound leader; a size 4 or 6 Kahle hook; and a 4-inch sucker minnow or a nightcrawler. A jig tipped with a minnow can also serve as a meat line. Clayton fishes his meat line by propping up the rod so the tip hangs over the side of the boat. Then he casts with another rod. When the meat line starts jerking, he immediately grabs the rod and sets the hook.

Clayton quickly convinced me of the merits of a meat line. He had no more than lowered the line over the side when the rod bowed over. Minutes

How to Rig and Fish a "Meat Line"

TIE a 30-inch, 6- to 8-pound mono leader to a 1- to 2-ounce Bottom Walker. Attach a size 4 or 6 Kahle hook; run it through the lips of a 4-inch sucker minnow.

LOWER the line to bottom, take up slack, then prop up the rod so the tip hangs over the side. Watch the tip as you fish with another line; when it jerks, set the hook.

later I netted his fish, a gorgeous 12-pounder. "Boat one, me none," he quipped. "With a meat line, the boat usually catches as many as I do."

"Best spot for a walleye over 10 pounds is a rocky, windswept point with a good food shelf near the old river channel," Clayton noted. "The big walleyes can rest in deep water and move up on the shelf to feed." Most of the big walleyes we caught on the trip were taken on exactly this type of spot.

"Another good spot, and one that most people ignore, is a mud hump surrounded by sand. It's got to be close to the old river channel. These spots don't look much good, but they hold a lot of big walleyes. See this hump over here" — Clayton pointed as we motored south out of New Town — "I've been catchin' big walleyes there all summer."

The hump was partially exposed because the water level of the reservoir was at least 10 feet below normal. "The mud's real hard, so the waves don't erode it," Clayton explained. "This hump's even got a few rocks on top — maybe that's why the walleyes like it so much."

We pulled up to the hump and started casting into the shallows. On my first cast, the jig stopped dead in midretrieve. I set the hook, missed, and pulled back my 4-inch redtail chub with an inch of skin torn back on each side. "Big walleye," Clayton deduced after examining the teeth marks. I cast back to the same spot, and again the jig stopped cold. This time, the hook stuck. On the first head shake, my rod tip jumped a foot. "Big walleye," Clayton reiterated. He was right — it was a 34-incher that weighed 12¼ pounds. The mud hump produced a 10 and two more 9s that afternoon, and a pair of 9s the next morning.

Sternberg with 12¼-pound walleye caught on mud hump

Clayton Folden's Prime Walleye Spots

ROCKY WINDSWEPT POINTS with extended lips are ideal feeding areas, especially if the point is near the old river channel.

MUD HUMPS near the old river channel, either partially exposed or submerged, draw big walleyes. The sand around the hump erodes, leaving only hard mud.

53

Folden with hefty string of 3- to 4-pound saugers

Walleye (left), sauger (middle), and saugeye (right)

Sauger

"Nice thing about guiding around here — you can always catch saugers, even when the walleyes won't bite. There's so many of 'em, we could never fish 'em out," Clayton observed.

"Saugers and walleyes are real similar fish. I don't do a whole lot of different things to catch 'em.

"Best advice is to fish deeper than you would for walleyes. The walleyes might be in 5 foot of water at the same time the saugers are in 25. I've caught 'em as deep as 80 foot. My favorite sauger technique is deep jigging.

"When I'm deep jigging, I troll real slow. Sometimes I have to use both the sea anchor and the trolling plates to go slow enough. I keep the jig as straight below the boat as I can. A heavy jig, about ½ ounce, works best. I don't know why — maybe 'cause it sinks faster — but I catch a lot more on a ½ ounce than on a ¼ ounce.

"When the jig hits bottom, I twitch it a little so it hops a few inches. Sometimes they'll really slam it when it's sinking — other times they just suck on it and you don't feel much other than a little more weight. If I feel a sharp hit, I set the hook right

away. Otherwise, I may wait a couple seconds to let them take it. If you don't keep the line straight up and down, you probably won't feel the hit and you can't get a good hook-set. Lotta guys drag the jig so far behind the boat they have no idea when a fish hits.

"White's a good sauger color, but they like chartreuse, too. Saugers are real greedy — they'll hit a jig tipped with a 4- or 5-inch minnow. But I usually put on two smaller minnows instead of a single big one — I'll hook more fish that way.

"In June, you can catch lots of saugers by trolling Long A Bombers in 20 to 25 foot. I like the baby-striper color — looks like a smelt.

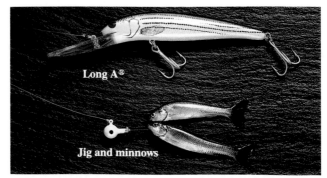

Folden's favorite sauger lures

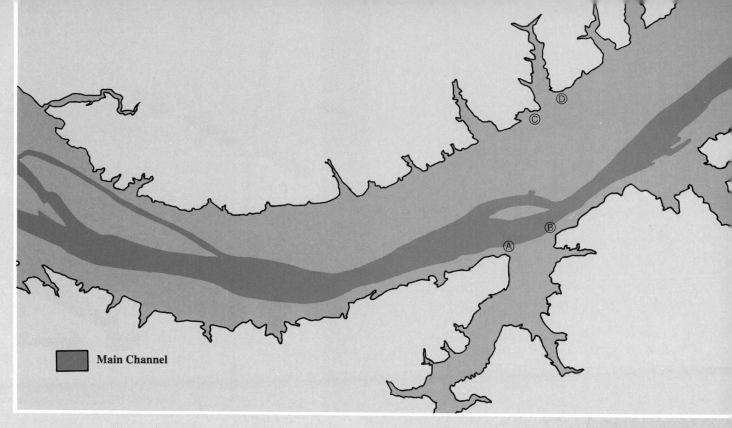

How Walleyes Relate to the Old River Channel

Structure adjacent to the old river channel is more likely to draw walleyes and saugers than structure some distance *away from it. Points A and B, for instance, would be much better choices than C and D, even though they might look very similar. At A and B the fish can rest in deep water, then easily move shallower to feed.*

Legend: Main Channel

"Bottom-bouncers work good, too. When the saugers are deep, it's a lot easier for the average guy to catch 'em on a bottom-bouncer than a jig. When the wind's blowin' and you're tryin' to fish a jig in 40 foot, it's tough to feel bottom.

"You can catch saugers on practically any sharp dropoff along the old river channel. They're almost always close to deep water. Boat control is real important when you're fishing these steep cuts. Lots of times, you'll find the saugers in 30 to 40 feet, and you have to hold your boat at exactly that depth.

"Best time for walleyes and saugers is late May to mid-June, then mid-October through November. One year we fished open water till December 19th. Had to break ice for each other, but we caught 'em in 25 to 40 foot. After the lake freezes up, we catch 'em in the tailrace [below Sakakawea]. We fish in the boat every month of the year."

When you set the hook in Lake Sakakawea, you're never really sure what's on the other end of the line. "Last year I was jigging for sauger in 50 foot of water when I felt a tap and set the hook," Clayton recollected. "The fish didn't move. I was using 4-pound line so I couldn't horse it. Twenty minutes later, I netted a 25-pound northern. She must have been down there chasing smelt. Still can't believe her teeth didn't cut the line."

Saugeyes, a walleye-sauger cross, also abound in Sakakawea. They grow considerably larger than pure saugers, often rivaling the size of the walleyes. An 11-pound 12-ounce saugeye was taken in 1984. "You'll catch saugeyes mixed right in with saugers," Clayton noted. "They're usually deeper than the walleyes."

Coho and chinook salmon are stocked in Sakakawea, but Clayton doesn't fish for them. "I won't buy a salmon stamp. We've got a good thing going here, and the salmon could mess it up. I wish they wouldn't have stocked 'em."

Clayton is a strong believer in catch-and-release fishing. "Used to be everybody kept all their fish," he recalled. "Now, most of us are throwin' some back. I keep saugers for eating, but I ask my customers to release the big walleyes unless they want to keep a trophy. I'd rather eat a sauger than a big walleye, anyway."

Besides, if Clayton kept all the big walleyes he catches, he'd risk a back injury lugging them up from the landing.

The TECHNIQUE for Walleyes

by Dick Sternberg

Dick Grzywinski's unique snap-jigging technique catches walleyes that ignore the usual methods

Ripping a jig through the weeds using the Technique

Dick Grzywinski deftly steered his boat through a dozen others scattered along the edge of a reef on Lake Winnibigoshish. "'Nuther one," he grunted as he set the hook on a chunky 3-pound walleye. It was his fifty-sixth of the day, and the time was only 11 a.m.

Every once in a while somebody in one of the other boats landed a walleye, but "the Grz" and his customers were hauling in five for every one they caught.

This scene has become a regular occurrence on "Big Winnie" in northern Minnesota. Baffled fishermen follow the Grz around and watch in amazement as he continues to reel in fish.

"It's the Technique," he'll tell you. Notice the capital *T*. That's because he considers it the *only* technique, at least on Big Winnie. And it's difficult to argue the point — it's not unusual for him to boat 100 or more walleyes a day on his guide trips.

The Technique is a fast jig-trolling method originated by the Grz, and practiced by him and a select group of his sidekicks. Most walleye experts advocate slow jigging, but the Grz has found that a fast, erratic jigging action will trigger walleyes that ignore slower offerings. Many envious anglers have studied the Technique and tried to duplicate it, but most have had only limited success. For a while, the would-be copycats were causing problems by following his boat too close and getting in the way, but most of them soon gave up out of frustration or embarrassment.

Despite his confidence in the Technique, the Grz isn't a one-method fisherman. In early spring, when the walleyes are up on shallow, rocky reefs, he cleans up by dropping anchor and pitching a slip-bobber rig baited with a lively ribbon leech. In lakes where the walleyes go deep in midsummer, he gets them by slow-trolling a slip-sinker rig baited with a leech or nightcrawler.

And walleyes aren't his only quarry. The rows of mounted fish on the walls of his living room, and the bulging photo album in his pickup camper, prove he's an accomplished multi-species angler. He spends a lot of time chasing northern pike, largemouth and smallmouth bass, bluegills, crappies, yellow perch, muskies, and even sturgeon. "Had to take down the picture of the wife on the living-room wall to make space for a big chinook salmon," he jokes. "On a cold winter night, I sit back and look at those fish and remember how much fun I had catching 'em."

But on many cold winter nights, the Grz isn't home staring at his walls; he's out ice fishing. In fact, he's an ice-fishing fanatic. He thinks nothing of walking two or three miles onto a lake in a raging blizzard, lugging a bucket of minnows and a 6-gallon pail full of tackle, and toting his Jiffy ice auger over his shoulder. He's been seen trudging off a lake with his beard completely covered with ice and the tips of his ears white from frostbite.

The Grz isn't sure how his nickname originated. It may have resulted from people being unable to pronounce his real name (the right way is *Ja-VIN-ski*), or from his bushy black hair and beard, which make him look like a grizzly bear. In spite of his

Dick Grzywinski

Home: *St. Paul, Minnesota*

Occupation: *Multi-species fishing guide; freight-dock worker.*

Dick Grzywinski — alias the Grz — doesn't fish the tournament circuit and hasn't gained the notoriety of other top walleye pros. But a few years back, in the Camp Fish Jamboree, a charity event sponsored by the In-Fisherman *magazine, he easily outdistanced a field of many of the Midwest's big-name anglers. The one-day tally for him and his guests was 97 walleyes and 54 northerns. In a more recent Jamboree, he took first-place honors for the biggest walleye with a 28-incher that he released.*

Very few guides take their work as seriously as the Grz. When he's on the water, there's no idle chatter. He's thinking about only one thing: catching fish. Instead of taking time out for lunch, he keeps on fishing, maybe chewing on a squashed, month-old candy bar he's found in his jacket pocket. He normally fishes until dark, so there's no time for dinner, either. On one week-long trip, he survived on only a loaf of bread and a jar of peanut butter. One night, for a special treat, he heated up a can of Dinty Moore beef stew.

And he's not about to let minor problems interfere with fishing. Once, while fixing his pickup just before a guide trip, he slashed his hand on a sharp piece of metal. The wound obviously required stitches, but he wasn't going to let it mess up the trip. "Just wrapped an old rag around it and went fishing," he explains. "Kept bleeding for a couple days. The doc chewed me out pretty good when I went in after the trip."

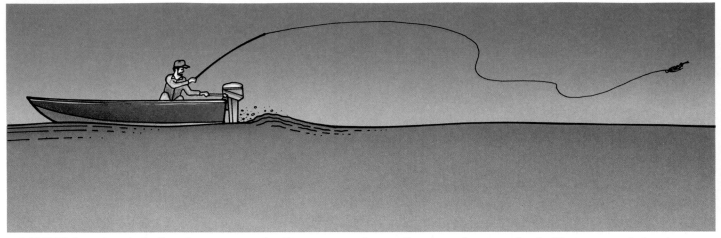

1. MOTOR into the wind, directly or at an angle. Cast the jig behind the boat; the distance you cast should be four or five times the water depth. Keep your rod aimed rearward and let the jig sink, but not to bottom.

3. RETURN your rod to the rearward position immediately after the wrist snap. This motion throws slack into the line and allows the jig to drop back and sink freely. Continue jigging this way as you troll.

formidable appearance, he's friendly, easygoing, and sincere. He loves to see his customers catch fish. In fact, if they aren't catching any, he'll hook the fish himself and then hand them the rod.

If you watch the Grz performing his magic act, it looks as if anyone should be able to do it. But many envious anglers have studied the Technique and tried to duplicate it, most with only limited success. Even the Grz has a hard time explaining exactly what he does. He's used the Technique so long it's become second nature.

On a recent fishing trip with him, I studied the Technique carefully, trying to analyze exactly what he does. First, he tied on a ¼-ounce jig, then tipped it with a minnow. After finding a suitable breakline, he flicked a cast out the back of the boat and let the jig sink a bit. Then he started ripping it with an extremely sharp wrist snap, while trolling at a speed most jig-trollers would consider too fast.

Asked how he knew how deep his jig was running, he replied, "Don't know for sure, but the water's 20 feet deep here, so I cast out as far as I can, then start jerkin'. I know I'm not on bottom because the jig's not pickin' up weeds. But I'm probably within a foot or two.

"The amount of line is real important," he advises. "If you let out too much, the jig won't lift off bottom, and you won't feel the strike. If you don't let out enough, you won't get down to the fish." From past experience, the Grz knows how far back to toss his jig for different water depths. After studying the Technique, I concluded that the right amount of line is about four to five times the depth.

The relatively fast trolling speed and sharp wrist snap are the two most obvious elements of the Technique. But there's another subtlety that could easily go unnoticed. The Grz snaps the jig, then immediately returns the rod to the initial position, allowing

2. SNAP the jig forward with a sharp wrist motion. Begin and end the jigging stroke at the rod positions shown above. On the snap, the jig darts forward and rises a short distance in the water.

4. SET the hook if you feel a slight twitch as the jig is sinking, or if the jig doesn't sink as expected. Often there is too much slack in your line to feel the strike, but when you snap the rod forward, you hook the fish.

the jig to sink on a slack line. Letting it sink this way has two advantages over normal jigging: the jig has a more erratic action, and you can set the hook more easily.

Normally, you would let the jig sink by lowering your rod slowly enough to maintain some tension, so you can feel the tap that signals a strike. But when you fish this way, the sink rate of the jig is slower and the action more controlled, so you may not trigger walleyes that aren't feeding. Also, strikes often come just as you start to lower the rod, so your arm may be too far forward to make a strong hook-set. But with the Technique, you immediately return the rod to the position where you started the snap, so your arm is always in position to set the hook.

How does the Grz detect strikes when the line is slack? Most of the time, he feels a very light tap, or maybe the jig doesn't sink the way it should.

Either way, he sets the hook with a powerful snap. Sometimes he doesn't feel the strike at all and gets surprised; when he snaps the jig forward, there's a fish on his line. Whether he feels the strike or not, the rod snap is strong enough to set the hook.

The Technique is not a one-lake method. "Works anywhere you have a long breakline," the Grz observes. "You can cover a lot of water in a hurry and locate the biters. And on quite a few lakes, it works from early spring through late fall.

"It's real good in weeds, too. In lots of lakes, that's where the walleyes are. If you try to drag a slip-sinker rig through a thick weedbed, you'll spend all day cleaning off your hook. But I can work my jig over the weed tops and call up the fish. And if I hook a weed, it'll usually come off on the next sharp jerk."

The Technique works best at depths of 15 feet or less, although the Grz uses it in water as deep as

25 feet. "Funny thing about Winnie — I catch walleyes from spring to fall at 7 feet. If it's calm, I can see bottom. Guys can't believe that the fish are that shallow, but I've caught 'em there for years. There's walleyes in deeper water too, but the shallow fish seem to bite better.

"I like a pretty good chop. Seems to turn the walleyes on. When it's calm, walleyes in shallow water may spook from the boat. When it's rough, you can troll right over 'em and they'll still bite."

The Grz doesn't use as much high-tech equipment as many of the top walleye pros, but he doesn't need it. His boat, a 16-foot Lund Rebel Special, is basic but very functional. It's deep-hulled enough to take rough water, yet light enough to operate with a 30-horsepower Suzuki outboard. In windy weather, he trolls with the Suzuki; in calm weather, with a 2-horsepower Evinrude. An electric motor wouldn't troll fast enough for the Technique. The boat is equipped with a Lowrance 2360 flasher and a Micronar 470 LCR, the latter a recent acquisition. "All I need to catch fish is a flasher," he maintains. "But it's a lot of fun watching 'em on the LCR.

"I like a long rod with a stiff butt and light tip. It's got to be stiff enough to snap the jig and set the hook, but the tip should be sensitive enough to feel a light strike. My favorite is a 7-foot Loomis IM6 spinning rod, model PR 842-25. With a short rod, you can't snap the jig enough. I still use my old Mitchell 300 reels — had 'em for thirty years now. I don't believe in expensive line. Eight- or ten-pound mill ends are good enough, but lately I've been using 6- or 8-pound Viking line. It's made in Japan, and it's a lot thinner than American line. Comes in 3000-yard spools for a buck twenty-nine. It's really tough — can't hardly break it. And it's good and clear."

The Grz's homemade feather jig, with fathead minnow

The jig is a special homemade number, with a bushy tail of hand-selected chicken feathers. "Takes me a long time to tie 'em," he bemoans. "Over an hour each. But it's worth it 'cause they catch more fish than anything you can buy. It really

The Grz hoists a 9-pound walleye

hurts when a sawbill [his nickname for a northern pike] snips one off. My favorite color for walleyes is chartreuse, but white works good too. When I run short of my own jigs I use a Fireball, made by Northland Tackle. It has a stubby hook that catches a lot of short-strikers.

"When the sawbills are really bad, I tie on a short wire leader. One of my customers gave me a spool of braided leader wire made by Berkley — it's real thin and doesn't seem to cut down on strikes.

"If the fish are bitin' good, I just use a plain jig. But if they're fussy I tip it with a minnow. I like fatheads 'cause they're tough. I can keep 'em in my live box for weeks. Best way to hook 'em is through the eyes. I get more bites that way, and they stay on the hook real good. But don't use the black ones with the warts on their head — they're males, and the walleyes just don't like 'em."

The Grz is a master at following structure, which may be the main thing that separates him from the competition. It's one thing to use the Technique, but it's another to use it in the precise depth zone where walleyes are congregated. Along the reef edges in Big Winnie, the zone may be as narrow as 1 foot; the exact depth depends on the time of year. If you fish slightly deeper or shallower, you won't catch a fish.

In a day when most walleye pros backtroll for precise boat control, the Grz trolls forward. "If I backtrolled fast enough to use the Technique, I'd sink my boat," he laughs. "It gets pretty rough on Winnie. The waves would come right over the transom.

"With the Technique, I always troll into the wind," he notes. "If you troll with the wind, you'll go too fast and you won't be able to control the boat. You can't stay on the structure. After I make a pass, I circle back, then make another."

The Grz seems to develop a jigging rhythm that suits the conditions. In shallow water, he trolls a little faster and snaps a little harder than in deep water. When fishing over weeds, he trolls even faster and snaps even harder, to keep the jig from sinking and fouling in the vegetation.

He doesn't have much time for fishing gadgets and short-cut methods. "I get a kick out of the guys that come up here with Color-C-Lectors and pH meters. All those things do is throw 'em off track. Never use scent on my bait either. A walleye doesn't strike because the bait smells good. He sees it trying to get away, and he smacks it. Lotta guys up here use scent — I can smell it a block away. But they're wastin' their time and money."

It's easy to understand why somebody would resort to those means when fishing alongside the Grz. When you're watching him haul in walleyes by the dozen and all you're getting is a suntan, you're looking for a little black magic.

Treasury of trophies: the Grz's scrapbook, growing thicker by the day

Getting Serious for Western Walleyes

by Jake Barnes

Since John McDonald started taking Columbia River walleye fishing seriously, he's boated over two hundred 10- to 15-pounders

In the southeast corner of Washington, not far downstream from Pasco, the Columbia River abruptly turns west to form the Oregon state line, before flowing powerfully 300 miles to the Pacific. This is farming country: flat, heavily irrigated land that often brews up big winds and serves them to the river.

John McDonald has been blown off the river for the past few days. But this day in August breaks calm, and he launches his 16-foot runabout at an impromptu ramp of river stone and rubble next to an irrigation pump. The lack of a state or commercial ramp on the Washington side of this mighty river says something about the broad view of fishing here, particularly the walleye fishing: the species is still not taken seriously, not yet.

McDonald heads downstream to a submerged island. Even from 500 yards away, its location is obvious: a half-dozen boats hover over and around it. As John approaches, several of the fishermen wave. He's well known on the Columbia. He's lectured and guided extensively, and it's no secret that a fisherman intent on big walleye would do well to look for good structure — or for John McDonald. Part of the price of success is that others have

followed him to his best spots; and now, whenever he goes to one of them, there's a crowd already waiting, as often as not.

John cuts the engine far upstream of the island and drifts toward it so the motor doesn't spook the fish. He describes the submerged island as though it were clearly visible. It's about a half mile long, and on the main-channel side is a hard bottom of rock and gravel. He intends to fish this side, zig-zagging along the 14- to 20-foot contours. At 18 feet, there's a transition from golfball-size rock to boulders about 1½ feet in diameter. The walleyes hide behind the boulders and dart out to grab food as it passes.

"In the middle of the island," he says, "there's a saddle that serves as a feeding station. We'll work across it, and pick up a fish just as the bottom drops off on this side." He pauses, then qualifies his forecast: "At least, we *should*. In the spring, I know the fish would be there, but now in this summer heat they're spread around. You have to put more time into finding fish, and that gives you less time to get them to bite."

John rigs up with a 6-foot, IM6 graphite casting rod that has a straight, two-hand grip; a baitcasting

---

John McDonald, Jr.

Home: *Pasco, Washington*

Occupation: *Paramedic, Pasco Fire Department*

John McDonald moved from Seattle to Pasco in 1974, to play minor-league baseball. He liked the area, got a job teaching school, and a few years later joined the fire department as a paramedic.

McDonald started bass-fishing the Columbia the year he arrived, and soon began to catch the incidental walleye. Most Pasco fishermen ignored walleyes, viewing them as strange, misguided creatures that had drifted downstream from large impoundments such as Lake Roosevelt, the site of the first Columbia walleye-stocking back in the 1940s. But McDonald was fascinated by the species. He read everything he could about walleyes, and quickly adapted midwestern techniques to the fast, windswept waters of the Columbia.

In 1977 McDonald got serious. He forsook bass to concentrate on walleyes. He began to catch 10-pound fish, raising some eyebrows in the bass-fishing crowd. He didn't own a depth finder, so he used contour maps and a lead-line to locate sand bars, islands, rubble piles, and other prime walleye structure. With that primitive equipment he acquired an intimate knowledge of the bottom, a familiarity that has paid off time and again. In tournaments he became unstoppable: at one competition in which 34 fish were boated, John and his fishing partner took 17 of them.

John's reputation soon began to grow. He was invited to join the pro staffs of Mister Twister and Lowrance Electronics. He guided for a few years, but guiding cut into his fishing time too much, so he quit in order to concentrate on perfecting his techniques and catching the biggest walleye the Columbia may hold. So far, his best is 15 pounds 15 ounces — only 2 pounds 1½ ounces shy of the state and river record.

reel (he prefers its drag system, strong and steady, to that of a spinning reel); and 8- to 10-pound premium mono. Nothing fancy — just simple, dependable gear suitable for detecting a walleye's light bite and then landing a big fish.

McDonald prefers baitcasting gear for Columbia River walleyes

He asks two of the anglers working the island how they've done and gets the thumbs-down signal. Although he prefers to jig, he decides to do some exploring with a spinner rig.

He makes three passes over the saddle of the island. Nothing. Where most fishermen would start to lose interest — like those in the six other boats haphazardly trolling this same structure — John becomes more intense. He begins a monologue on the bottom conditions, as if he were reading a teletype message transmitted through his rod. Carefully studying his Lowrance X-15B graph, he calls out minor dropoffs and big rocks. After every pass he checks his worm, tossing it away if it doesn't look fresh.

After several passes, John connects with a 6-pound fish, which he brings in with little fanfare. To him, a walleye that size is just an average catch. It takes at least a 10-pounder to get him excited.

As we continued to fish, McDonald explained his methods for finding and catching Columbia River walleyes.

"Walleyes in the Columbia aren't much different than walleyes in other big rivers," he contended. "They move up to the dams in late fall and stay there through the winter until they spawn in spring. Then they filter back downstream and by summer are scattered in deeper water.

"The upstream migration of walleyes starts after the first frost in September. Fishing below the dams is excellent until the really cold weather hits, then it gets tough.

"Action at the dams picks up again in January. You can catch smaller fish, mostly males, until early March. Most of 'em run 3 to 8 pounds. The best springtime spots are eddies and other slack-water areas formed by islands and points projecting into the main channel. I usually find the fish in 8 to 18 feet of water.

"In most years, runoff is heavy from mid-March to early April; the water turns chocolate brown and fishing is lousy. I like to fish just when the river starts to clear. That's when the big females from 8 pounds on up start to hit."

But fishing slows again in late April, when spawning begins. Walleyes start to bite again around Memorial Day as they recuperate from spawning and begin settling into their summertime locations. As a rule, McDonald feels that summertime walleyes in the Columbia will hold in fairly deep water adjacent to structure. For brief periods, they move onto the structure to feed. Besides sunken islands, his best summertime spots are large gravel bars extending out from shore.

Most mornings, he starts fishing about 14 to 16 feet down and works deeper as the sunlight intensifies.

"I like to fish jigs whenever I can," McDonald says. He appreciates the delicate sense a good jig fisherman must have to detect a walleye's bite, and he enjoys the thrill of feeling the take the instant it occurs.

Years ago, he started his walleye fishing on the Columbia with the ¼-ounce jigs popular in the Midwest. He soon discovered, however, that he needed more weight to stay deep in the strong currents of the river. So he went to bigger sizes, his typical jig now being a ¾-ouncer. Sometimes he fishes a ½-ounce jig, and he resorts to a 1-ounce magnum job when the river is running fast.

In his early days on the river, McDonald rigged his jigs with a twin-tail plastic grub and a nightcrawler (minnows are prohibited on the river, and leeches unavailable). He'd jig vertically over good walleye cover, picking the jig up 6 to 18 inches and then letting it gently flutter to the bottom. Most often the fish would take on the drop, and soon he developed that sixth sense for detecting the subtle tap that signals a walleye hit. But despite his skill and persistence, he was missing a lot of fish. "One afternoon I hooked only one walleye out of a dozen strikes," he recalled. "That's when I decided to try a trailer."

Rigging a worm with a trailer hook was a trick he first picked up from kokanee salmon fishing. Later, he found that walleye experts in the Midwest and South were doing the same thing. He liked to run his trailer hook 4 to 5 inches behind the jig head, so it could be inserted well back in the nightcrawler. The crawler would then trail straight to the rear without bunching up. The problem, though, was that vertical jigging with a long trailer line caused it to tangle frequently on the main line ahead of the jig.

To solve the tangling problem, he added a significant new feature. He rigged the trailer on 20-pound mono and ran it *inside* the length of a 4-inch twin-tail grub. The stiff, heavy mono helped keep the hook directed straight back, and so did the grub. "Since I started using this setup on my jigs," he says, "the trailer hook catches 70 percent of the walleyes."

The most productive colors for jig heads, according to McDonald, are chartreuse, fluorescent green, and orange, but salmon and steelhead like the orange so well that he rules it out to avoid catching them. In the spring, he uses chartreuse twin-tails; in summer, smoke color with glitter; in fall, smoke with glitter, purple, and chartreuse.

Electric motor controls drift along contour

Most of the time, McDonald jigs vertically while drifting with the current. He uses a 3-horsepower transom-mount electric motor to control the drift, generally keeping the boat over 18 to 26 feet of water. The right time for jigging, he says, is when the fish are concentrated in spring and fall, or when he's already pinpointed a school by exploratory trolling with a plug or a spinner-worm rig.

How McDonald Rigs His Trailer-Hook Jig

LAY a length of 20-pound mono along the hook shank and collar of an Erie jig head; form a loop as shown.

PASS the free end of the mono around the collar and through the loop four times. Tighten and trim.

RUN the mono through the eye of a size 4 barbed-shank hook; tie as before. The mono is now 4 inches long.

THREAD the trailer into the front of a 4-inch twin-tail grub (left), then out between the tails (right).

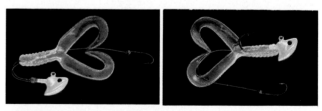
INSERT the jig hook where the mono goes through the grub (left). Seat the grub on the jig collar (right).

HOOK a nightcrawler as shown. The mono has a little slack; the shank of the trailer is hidden in the worm.

65

In windy weather, or when the walleyes are scattered, McDonald resorts to trolling with plugs. "I don't really like trolling," he says. "I troll to find schools of walleyes, then I usually go back to jigging." His favorite trolling plugs are Hot'n Tots, Wiggle Warts, Fat Raps, and Mann's 20+ and 30+. He generally trolls upstream in 6 to 20 feet of water, paying out as much as 70 feet of line to

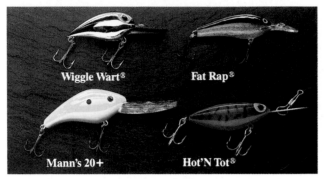

McDonald's pick of walleye trolling plugs

reach bottom. He also uses plugs when he finds walleyes chasing baitfish in the shallows, but then he casts rather than trolls.

McDonald also trolls with a spinner-worm rig when conditions aren't right for jigging. Like his jigs, his spinners are rigged with trailer hooks. The main spinner hook goes through the crawler's nose; the trailer hook is buried toward the rear of the worm. He uses size 4 willowleaf and Indiana blades, which will run closer to the bottom than the broader Colorado blades. Hammered nickel is his favorite finish, but he also uses copper (especially on dark days) and brass. If the water is

discolored, a chartreuse Indiana blade is his choice. He dresses the spinner with about nine colored beads — red, green, and silver in various combinations — threaded on the line directly behind the spinner clevis. "Sometimes it makes a big difference when you change the color combination," he observes. "When I find a combination that works, I'll stick with it until the fish quit biting."

Two to four split-shot ahead of the rig keep it down near the bottom. The shot are large, about ⅛ ounce apiece. When he's fishing over a rocky bottom, he rigs up a special weight, called a "slinky," to avoid snags. He ties off one end of a section of hollow parachute cord, about ¼ inch in diameter, then pours shot in the other end and ties it off as well. The amount of shot varies from ¼ to ⅜ ounce, depending on the conditions. The sinker hangs on a short monofilament dropper from a three-way swivel; the spinner trails the swivel on a 12- to 24-inch snell. "This sinker really slips over the rocks," McDonald says. "It's more snagless than anything else I've seen."

McDonald works the spinner-worm rig at a slow troll with his electric motor. He trolls downstream, so the rig will run close to the bottom with less line out. Keeping the line short makes it easier to feel the bottom and detect strikes.

John believes an outboard will spook walleyes, so he's careful not to motor over a spot he plans to fish. "When I finish a downstream run and want to motor back up for another, I crank up the outboard and swing wide around the fish, 50 yards or more to the side."

How McDonald Makes His Slinky Rig

PULL (1) the fiber core out of a 4- to 8-inch piece of parachute cord. (2) Wrap string several times around one end of the cord, and tie with three half-hitches. (3) Pour lead shot through a straw and into the cord; the amount of shot can vary from ¼ to ⅜ ounce. (4) Tie the other end. (5) Tie a mono dropper to the slinky and attach the other end to a three-way swivel, along with the main line and a leader rigged with a spinner-worm combo.

As John continues his lengthy on-the-water seminar, it soon becomes obvious that he is a serious student of walleye behavior and a versatile walleye angler. His extensive knowledge came from spending long hours on the river and from reading everything about walleyes he could lay his hands on. By the time the seminar is finished, it is almost dark.

The following morning, the winds are up strong. The submerged island John favors is topped with 4-foot whitecapped waves. Fishing there would be an ordeal. He heads back towards Pasco, to a bend in the river providing some shelter, and launches the boat. The best structure here, he says, is the rubble beneath a navigational buoy. The river has many spots like this one: rock and gravel heaped up under a buoy and coming nearly to the surface, with surrounding water 40 to 70 feet deep. The rock and the current break give baitfish a place to collect, and walleyes a good spot for feeding.

A dozen other fishermen have come to this same place today, probably because of the wind, so the buoy looks like a slalom pole in the world's slowest powerboat race. John trolls a spinner, then switches to a deep-diving plug. He takes two small fish, which aren't enough to hold him here. He reels in and heads downstream.

Although everyone fishing this stretch today has made the same initial decision — to fish the structure near the buoy — John is the only one to grow dissatisfied and go exploring. He heads to a ¼-mile-long gravel bar where he's taken fish before, and ties on a spinner rig. Carefully, he begins to troll over the structure, controlling his spinner depth and direction with judicious bursts from the electric motor.

From 12 feet on top, the bar slopes to 40 feet in the main channel. About halfway down is a transition from egg-sized gravel to boulders as large as 3 feet in diameter. No fish are visible on the graph, but McDonald figures they're sitting behind the rocks. On his first pass he trolls the shallower part of the bar, then on successive runs he moves closer and closer to the main channel, working the boulders.

"There should be fish here," he comments — the monologue again.

Three or four, five passes later, over this same unseen field of rock, a big fish hits. John pops the rod to set the hook. The walleye makes a good run, then settles into a steady pull.

As the fight goes on, the fish shaking its head and making several more uncontrollable runs, John's monologue increases in volume and fervor. Despite having taken more than 200 walleyes weighing

McDonald turns a 10-pounder loose on the Columbia

over 10 pounds each, he's lost no enthusiasm for his sport. Finally, ten minutes after the strike, another 10-pound-plus walleye glides exhausted into the net.

Carefully, John removes the hook and eases the walleye over the side. Grasping it by the tail, he works it back and forth through the water until it revives. Then, with swish of the tail and a splash, it disappears.

John McDonald no longer kills big fish, but releases them to be caught another day. The philosophy that now is commonplace in the ranks of trout fishermen is making slow inroads among talented walleye anglers like McDonald.

"There are still plenty of walleyes," he says, "but I, for one, have to work a lot harder to find them than I used to. Now a local coalition of Indian tribes wants permission to sell the fish they catch incidentally in gillnets. They can already sell them in Oregon. I've seen as many as twenty walleyes come out of an Indian's net. The incidental catch could easily be large enough to jeopardize the fish population here."

This from a man who is a native Alaskan, and whose mother is a full-blooded Aleut.

"There's not a lot of natural walleye reproduction in the middle and lower Columbia," McDonald concludes, "and the state doesn't want to stock walleyes because anglers think they eat loads of salmon and steelhead smolts, despite studies showing otherwise. So we need to put these trophy walleyes back for a successful spawn. Take a few small ones to eat, but release the others. They're just too valuable to kill."

Walleye Tips

Gary Howey
Sliding Sinker Stop

Lindy Rigs or other pre-tied slip-sinker rigs are standard in fishing live bait for walleyes. But these rigs have some drawbacks. The leader inevitably gets scuffed up, so you have to cut off the hook and retie, often leaving your leader too short. Most slip-sinker rigs have three knots that are potential weak spots. Gary Howey, a guide and publisher of "The Outdoorsman" newspaper, from Hartington, Nebraska, ties his own rigs using rubber stops made by Northland Tackle. The knot attaching the hook is the only knot required. If the leader gets scuffed, he snips off the hook, reties, and slides the stop a few inches up the line. Another advantage: the leader length can be adjusted to suit different fishing conditions by simply moving the stop.

THREAD on a slip-sinker. Insert your line through the wire ring that comes with the stop, then slide the stop off the wire onto your line. Tie on your hook.

Jim Crowley
Plastic Worms for Walleyes

Jim Crowley, a Hunting and Fishing Library subscriber and resident of Fayetteville, New York, fishes big walleyes in logs and brush using plastic worms. Jim discovered the technique after losing a pile of jigs in a log-strewn Canadian lake. Out of frustration, he tied on an 8-inch worm rigged Texas-style and started catching 5- to 9-pounders. The technique has proven to be a consistent early-season producer in Canadian lakes. Jim's favorite worm colors are blue, lime-green, and purple.

ED IMAN is a well-known Columbia River fishing guide from Gresham, Oregon, and a member of the Mariner National Fishing Team. Ed used his diving worm harness to take this 17 pound 5 ounce walleye, only 3 ounces shy of the Oregon state record.

Ed Iman
Diving Worm Harness

Spinner-nightcrawler rigs are one of the top walleye producers, but the sinkers normally used to get them deep snag easily on a rocky bottom. Ed Iman solves the problem by using deep-diving plugs to pull the spinner rig down. He attaches the spinner rig to a bright-colored plug with the hooks removed. The plug will reach depths of 15 to 25 feet and will seldom snag. The bright color of the plug attracts fish to the spinner rig.

REMOVE the hooks from a deep-diving plug such as a Hot Lips (shown), attach a snap-swivel to the split-ring on the front hook hanger, then clip the spinner rig into the snap. This way, you can easily change spinners.

Jack Schneider
Luminescence for Walleyes

Luminescent (glow-in-the-dark) lures are known to catch more walleyes under low-light conditions than ordinary lures. They work especially well around dusk or dawn, at night, in stained water, or on cloudy or windy days when light penetration is reduced. But good luminescent lures are hard to find, so Jack Schneider, a tournament walleye fisherman from Star Prairie, Wisconsin, doctors his lures with Firefly Luminescent Film, manufactured by Blue Fox Tackle Company. Schneider maintains that a little glow is better than a lot. "A lure glowing like a neon sign will scare fish away," he says. He applies a small piece of the film to the side of a crankbait or minnow plug, to a jig head, or to jigging lures used

for ice fishing. The film comes in medium and low intensity. Schneider uses the medium intensity for water of low to moderate clarity; the low intensity for water of high clarity.

Max Berry
Columbia River Jig

Max Berry, a Hunting and Fishing Library subscriber and veteran fisherman from Boise, Idaho, uses a unique rig for Columbia River walleyes. It consists of a jig head rigged with a plastic twin-tail grub, and a trailing keeper hook with a nightcrawler. The crawler draws more strikes, and the fish are usually hooked on the trailer.

RIG a ⅝-ounce Erie jig head with a 4-inch chartreuse twin-tail grub. Force the eye of a 2/0 keeper hook over the point of the jig hook, then push the keeper into the crawler's head and the hook point into its side.

Elden Bailey
Jigs in the Brush

Walleyes spend a lot of time in brushy cover, but fishing the brush is frustrating because of constant snags. Elden Bailey, a radio fishing show host and state walleye-tournament champion from Lawrence, Kansas, solves the problem by adding monofilament brushguards to small, plastic-bodied jigs. With a brushguard, the jig will slide through the brush with few snags.

INSERT both ends of a 2-inch piece of 20-pound monofilament line into the opening where the jig goes through the front of the plastic body. Push the loop formed by the line under the barb of the hook.

Jerry Anderson
Cut Bait Jigging

A jig-and-minnow combination is deadly for walleyes, but the fish often strike short, gouging the minnow's tail and missing the hook. Jerry Anderson, a Manufacturers' Walleye Council tournament champion from Onamia, Minnesota, tips his jigs with cut minnows when the fish are hitting short. With the shortened minnow, the fish usually strikes far enough forward to get hooked. Cutting the minnow also gives off extra scent which helps attract walleyes. The technique works equally well for open-water fishing and ice fishing.

CUT the minnow diagonally to remove its head. Using a plain ⅟₁₆- to ⅛-ounce jig, insert the hook into the front of the cut portion, then out through the skin just ahead of the dorsal fin.

Northern Pike & Muskellunge

Ted Jowett

Home: *Winnipeg, Manitoba*

Occupation: *Fishing and hunting guide*

Ted Jowett fishes and hunts — and helps others to do so — some 300 days a year. He starts in the long Manitoba winters, dangling lines through the ice for pike and walleyes. Springtime is bear season: he's busy preparing and setting out forty baits, big oil drums filled with fish, bread, and honey. He also schedules in some early walleye trips — fishing in the morning, hunting in the afternoon. June is for pike and for big channel cats, 20 pounds plus, in the Winnipeg River. July and August finds him guiding in northern Manitoba, beyond the tree line, where pot-bellied lakers hang near the surface and pike grow as long as church pews.

Come autumn, the pace really picks up. In September, Jowett fishes walleyes; by October he's hunting geese, while continuing with the walleyes — leaving home at 3 in the morning, returning at 11 at night, seven days a week. He guides bow hunters for deer from late October through November; mercifully, the goose guiding

The One-Two Punch for Pike

by Nat Franklin Jr.

Ted Jowett uses European dead-bait methods and big artificial lures to outwit Canadian monster pike

On a morning early in June, Ted Jowett launches his boat at a ramp in the heart of Whiteshell Provincial Park, in southeast Manitoba. Daybreak came at 4 a.m.; and now, only 9, it feels like lunchtime. The temperature has wasted no time hitting the mid-90s. The past two weeks have been record-breakers, nearly 100 degrees every afternoon — a condition Jowett says will make the pike fishing a real challenge, since mature northerns are cold-water fish by nature.

A bush plane floats at a dock nearby; and beside it, incongruously, a swimmer dog-paddles in almost tropical water. Jowett's water thermometer registers

halts with the first big freeze around November first. Finally, sometime in November, the ice is solid enough for him to head out with his frostbite angling customers again.

"I guess it's a little hard on my system," Jowett says. "If I ever get tired of it, I'll just quit and go back to the machine shop. But I'll never get tired of it."

The machine shop: before becoming a guide, he worked ten-hour shifts on a 100-ton punch press. He also did stints as a farm worker, landscaper, construction worker, and delivery-truck driver. But he'd grown up fishing and hunting with his father and wanted to make a career of it, so eventually he got a sales job at a tackle shop in Winnipeg. There, he started to sign up customers for guide trips on his days off.

In eight years of guiding, Jowett and his parties have taken seventy pike over 20 pounds and hundreds in the teens. The biggest was just over 27 pounds. In 1987, Jowett competed in Manitoba's first pike tournament ever, a two-day event on Paint Lake. Out of a crowded field of 400 entrants, both amateur and professional, he finished in first place.

80 at the surface — with the calendar start of summer still more than two weeks away. This will be his first pike trip since the end of bear season, and the fishing conditions could scarcely be more unusual, the pike behavior harder to predict. But Jowett is prepared for almost any eventuality. In the boat he's got a styrofoam-lined box prickling with jerkbaits, spinnerbaits, and standard bucktail spinners, plus a big cooler packed with dead smelt and other baitfish on ice.

Jowett displays his lures and baits

Dead bait? In this instance, it's not the result of overcrowding or bad water in a minnow bucket, but deliberate choice. Though Ted Jowett is an all-around pike angler, a pragmatist who gives stubborn fish whatever they want on a given day, his specialty is tempting them out with stone-cold, stiff-as-a-board dead bait. To the uninitiated, fishing with any baitfish that isn't alive, well and wriggling might seem a form of madness. But not to Jowett, nor to any of his pike-fishing clients. Jowett has been one of the first North American anglers to adopt the deadly dead-bait techniques imported from Europe and the British Isles.

One reason for bringing dead bait along today is purely regulatory: here in the Whiteshell Park, live bait isn't allowed. If you want to feed the northerns real meat — and there are times when this will work much better than any artificial — then your only option is a dead "live" bait.

But even if given a choice, Jowett would still do his trophy-pike fishing with dead bait, at least in the early season. Northerns are far more inclined to take a dead bait than a live one during those initial weeks of fishing after the opener. Tons of baitfish die in winter when lakes and rivers are shrouded with ice, and the pike get in the habit of scrounging — *scavenging* — these inert, easy meals. Come spring, the bottom is a veritable smorgasbord of dead bait-fish, and pike continue to feed on them well past the spawning period. Artificials? Until the water warms more and the larder of dead protein runs low, few trophy northerns are about to go chasing any zippy chunks of chrome or polystyrene.

On this late-spring day, the spawn is only three weeks past; but since then, the water has warmed much faster than normal. Jowett makes a final check of his bait and lure supplies, then cranks up and heads across Big Whiteshell Lake.

His boat is a Lund Alaskan, an 18-footer built of heavy .100-inch aluminum. Three pedestal seats for his clients form a row along the centerline; he takes out a seat or two on days when he's guiding fewer fishermen. Aft is a fourth seat, offset to one side, where he sits to operate the electric motor and the tiller-control outboard. Along each side of the hull is a large rod locker. Jowett helped Lund design this particular layout, so it's ideal for his style of fishing. His 70-horse tiller-operated out-board is more powerful than any tiller model available in the U.S.

The lake this morning is utterly flat, not a whisper of breeze. The water is clear, visibility several feet, with a thin saffron layer of pollen adrift on the sur-face. The sun beats down brighter and brighter; for dead-baiting, Jowett would favor wind and clouds. He sets his jaw.

"I have to be on a high note all the time" — so goes his credo of successful guiding — "a positive note. If I wake up thinking I can't catch fish, I've still got to cheer you up. So I think: just one fish, that one big trophy. If we can just present the bait properly, we might tag that one big fish."

Out comes the tackle. His rods are 6½-footers, baitcasting, medium-heavy action. The length is a

compromise, a reasonably happy one: he readily acknowledges that a longer rod, 8½ feet, would be the ideal for lobbing dead-bait rigs, while a shorter rod, 5½ feet, would be handier for "throwing wood." He supplies all the tackle for his fisher-men, and the compromise rods reduce the clutter on deck. He spools his reels with 17-pound mono. Artificials are rigged on 30-pound wire leaders with sturdy cross-lock snaps. For dead bait, he assembles quick-strike rigs — European devices, to his mind "the greatest invention since the telephone."

Big Whiteshell has a maximum depth of only 20 feet, so the pike cannot go deep to escape the heat. Jowett believes he will find them at a depth of 8 to 12 feet. The spot he's picked now is an extensive bed of cabbage; in places it's already grown to the surface, but most of it remains at least a few inches below, leaving plenty of room to slip a lure over it.

He starts with a big jerkbait, a Teddie, heaving it with thick forearms into openings on the outside edge of the weedbed. On the retrieve, he points the rod straight ahead and makes the lure dart a foot or so at a time, by jerking the rod tip downward until it almost touches the water. The rod stays below horizontal at all times. Because of the longer rod, he stands on one of the rod lockers to gain extra height above the water.

Jowett keeps rod aimed at jerkbait on retrieve

Sometimes he makes short jerks to the side. The big mistake he sees most anglers commit is sweep-ing the rod so far to the side they can't set the hooks when a pike hits. It takes a good hard jab, or a se-ries of them, to pull the wood through a trophy pike's teeth and sink the barbs. When a fish hits, Jowett hauls the rod up high and hard, rather than trying to set the hook by jerking farther down or sideways.

Several pike slam his Teddie, then whip and buck through the water like overloaded leaf springs on a potholed road. A few 5-pounders, a 6, plus any number of smaller fish. He releases each one of them carefully, bending low over the side of the boat with his pliers.

Jowett is a forceful advocate of catch-and-release pike fishing. His stern pronouncements on putting trophy fish back would win the admiration of any no-kill trout nut. "Up at Nejanilini [in far northern Manitoba, where he guides in midsummer] everyone wants to take home just one trophy pike. But I say, look, pike grow slow up here, they put on maybe a pound a year. If 50 guys come up in a season and take out a 20-pound fish, you're knocking off a thousand years of growth, just like that. Pretty soon, you're going to have no trophies left in the lake."

To avoid injuring pike, he unhooks them without lifting them fully out of the water. If a picture is to be taken, he waits until the camera is ready before pulling the fish up. He weighs a trophy pike without harm by slipping a special weighing sack under it in the water, then lifting the sack out and attaching it quickly to the scales. The sacks are available commercially; they're actually fine-weave slings with a pocket at each end to keep the head and tail of the fish from slipping out. Landing nets should not be used for this purpose, since the coarse mesh will cut into a fish and scrape off the slime.

Sack permits weighing and releasing pike unharmed

In search of bigger game, Jowett switches to a spinnerbait for casting way back in, right over the cabbage. He likes to fish this type of lure just under the surface, so it makes a bulge on top as it travels along. His preference is a tandem-blade spinnerbait, which has two blades on a single arm, one behind the other. This design has greater lift than a single-blade model, because of the double water resistance; it's much easier to fish on the surface.

Jowett's favorite warm-weather hardware

He holds his rod high and reels just fast enough to keep the lure from falling into the cabbage. When it reaches an opening, he slows the retrieve to let it drop a short way beneath the surface.

"Unbelievable" : Jowett's terse reaction when his first spinnerbait pike of the post-bear hunt season clobbers the burbling lure. A few others take a swipe at it too, though not as many as hit the jerkbait. Jowett decides to cover more water, and trolls for a while along the outer edge of the weedbeds. He trails the a big bucktail spinner about 20 yards behind the boat.

A half hour of this, with no sawlog pike to show for it, and Jowett decides to pack it in. The heat has definitely soured the fishing. A couple of years ago these same waters produced pike of 25½, 23½, 22 and several in the teens in one day of fishing.

Reasoning that the effects of the heat wave may not be as great in moving water, Jowett loads the boat and hits the road northward. On the way through Whiteshell Park, birches and aspens glow in early pale-green leaf; broods of newly hatched teal and mallards swim in ditches along the berm. Everywhere in the park, water is low: rain has been scant, and forest fires blackened some areas in the middle of May, several months earlier than the usual fire season. "Spots that used to have good cabbage with water on top are dead," says Jowett. He's discussing the river, the Winnipeg, as he gestures toward its flat, lakelike waters at a launch ramp. "This low water has really been messing us up the last few years."

The boat skims upriver to a narrows bounded by huge mounds of pink granite. The river stays flat here, no whitewater, but through the constriction a visible flow powerfully uncurls. "When the water was normal, I used to make guys get out of the boat before I went through," he explains. "The water was so fast it was a tough run." He snakes smoothly through, and then up several more miles to a dam with a brick powerhouse on top.

Surprisingly strong currents thump from a series of gates beneath. A hundred yards downstream, a necklace of oil drums strung on a thick steel cable keeps boats from running any closer. Jowett's motor churns upcurrent, blaring like a mandrill. He zips across the cable, having raised the lower unit at the last instant, pressing a button at the tip of the tiller, timing it perfectly. The button is normally the kill switch but Jowett rewired it, to avoid turning around backward to operate the tilt switch on the engine itself.

"I know these people here," he points out. Up on the dam, a worker in a hardhat gives him a high sign.

With his electric motor, Jowett maneuvers near the last gate, where the current eddies out in a slack pocket beside a natural outcrop of granite. Once in position, he sets to work with the tackle.

Jowett's version of the quick-strike rig consists of 18 inches of Sevenstrand braided-steel wire, 30-pound test, with two treble hooks attached. The hook on the front tip of the wire is a size 6 or 8; the other one, which slides along the wire, is a size 10. Jowett prefers bronzed trebles, not stainless, since they'll rust out of a fish's jaw if a break-off should occur. The wire is connected to his line with a large swivel. On the line itself, a slip-bobber is rigged.

The dead bait is usually a mooneye, smelt, tullibee or sucker. It should measure 6 to 12 inches long; big pike generally go for the bigger baits within this range.

Jowett inserts the front hook first, on the top side of the baitfish straight above the gill opening. The rear hook is inserted into the body at the front of the dorsal fin; since the hook slides on the wire, the rig adjusts to baitfish of any size.

Rod inclined to the rear, both hands on the grip, Jowett takes a long, hard look at the rolling water. The hook-studded baitfish hangs in air, slowly revolving: on lighter tackle, it wouldn't be a half-bad catch.

He launches it smoothly toward the edge of the current emerging from the gate. The throw is short, an easy lob that won't separate the bait from the hooks. The bait sinks until the bobber stop on the line draws snug against the bobber; Jowett feeds a bit of line as the rig drifts on the current, so the bobber has just enough slack to stand up straight. The rule on setting bait depth, he says, is to put it either halfway to the bottom or within 2 feet of the bottom. In winter and early spring, he gets 90 percent of his pike close to the bottom, but once the water warms up he varies his depth more.

Another tip: don't let your bobber get farther than 35 feet from the boat, or hook-sets will be tough because of the sharp angle formed in the line at the bobber. When the rig starts to drift too far away in the current, he reels in a few yards of line and lets it drift again. Occasionally he starts over with a new cast, though casting is best kept to a minimum so the bait isn't torn loose.

"I usually set the hook within a few seconds after the bobber goes down and moves off," says Jowett. "If the bobber's moving toward me, I wait a little longer. Your hooking percentage is best when the fish is swimming away.

"A pike will take a bait in its mouth crosswise, and the idea is to set the hook before it gets the bait aimed down its gullet and starts to swallow." With a single-hook rig, you miss too many fish if you strike early: the hook may not be in the fish's mouth till the bait is swallowed, or nearly so. But with the quick-strike rig, one hook or the other will generally be in striking position whenever the pike picks

How to Tie and Fish a Quick-Strike Rig

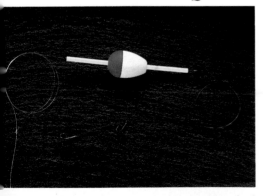

THREAD on slip-bobber, add swivel and wire leader, slip on size 10 treble, crimp on size 6 or 8 treble.

HOOK the baitfish with main treble above the gill opening; sliding treble at the front of dorsal fin.

LOB-CAST with a smooth sidearm motion to avoid snapping the bait off the hook.

up the bait. If you wait too long to strike, the fish will get the hooks deep. That means it usually won't give you a great battle; nor will you be able to turn it loose uninjured.

A flutter of the bobber, then it heels over and abruptly vanishes. For a moment, the eggshell color of the sunken float shines up through the scum and bubbles drifting on the surface. Jowett holds off, rod pointed low, but not for long: the period of grace seems five or six seconds, at most.

He sets the hooks with a flick of the wrists. With a quick-strike rig, a powerful hook set is not necessary and may even rip the hooks out. The fish affixes itself to the current, heading for the oil drums and deep realms beyond. In five minutes or so, the stiff rod and Jowett's thumb on the spool take a toll. Fifty yards out, the fish starts to tire, thrashing on the surface and allowing Jowett to work it back to the boat.

Jowett goes after the hooks with his pliers. One treble is caught in the acute angle of the jaw; the other hangs unattached. Frequently, Jowett says, both hooks will be in the fish, one on each side of the mouth. A hook may have ripped loose in this case: the pike is a fine one, close to 15 pounds.

In the course of this scorching northern day Jowett catches — and releases — at least a score of good-sized pike from the chutes and eddies below the dam. Most fall to his quick-strike rig, but several hit jerkbaits and spinners. "You get the more aggressive fish with the jerkbait," he says. "But the bigger ones go for the dead bait."

He recalls the time when he was guiding for catfish on the river, and his client decided he wanted to catch a pike. Jowett rigged him up with a quick-strike rig and a dead bait, and tossed anchor below the powerhouse. The anchor was necessary because he didn't have his electric motor along — he doesn't ordinarily use it when catfishing. Within seconds, the client's bobber shot under the surface and he set the hook. "How does it feel?" Jowett wanted to know, as the fish ran with the rig. "Like a 20-pounder," said the client, who'd been hauling in catfish about that size.

At that instant, a sudden release of heavy water rumbled from the dam gates, washing the pike right under the boat. Jowett got a glimpse of the fish and saw it would go far more than 20 pounds — maybe 15 pounds more, in fact. But on its way past the anchor rope, one of the trebles snagged; the other tore loose from the fish. Finale of saga — or so Jowett figured. Only minutes later, the former catfisherman tied into another pike. This one came aboard: all 21 pounds of it.

Jowett lands hefty pike below Winnipeg River dam

Besides dams, Jowett's favorite springtime spots for fishing dead bait are the mouths of creeks and backwaters, and openings into shallow bays where the pike have spawned. Dead bait will take fish in summer too, though the fish generally like something that moves faster then, and artificials are more productive in most cases. Also, weeds are a problem when fishing in summer; to avoid snags with a dead bait, you're limited to fishing the edges of the beds. If you do fish dead bait in the warmer months, Jowett recommends the "high-percentage spots — rocky points or any place along shore where pike might concentrate or funnel past." Fall is good for dead bait, though he's less likely then to use a quick-strike rig than a big bucktail jig baited with a dead sucker.

Toward the end of our trip, the heat finally breaks. A cold rain falls briefly in the morning. The midday air temperature is 40 degrees lower than the day before; the river temperature plummets to 66. But when Jowett is fishing for pike, cold fronts don't bother him. "We're after one fish," he announces. "We can get him anytime. We just put the bait right in front of a fish."

He puts it there, and he catches plenty.

How to "Sting" a Muskie

by Greg Breining

Premier muskie guide Don Pursch has caught dozens of 30- to 40-pounders with his deadly jerkbait technique

Don Pursch digs through a pile of hooks and chunks of wood the size of hammer handles lying on the deck of his boat. "See this?" he says, "This is Old Sting."

Old Sting is a weather-beaten, tooth-worn chunk of wood that once would have been recognized as a Suick, a popular jerkbait. It's an ungainly plug about 8 inches long with squarish corners and a crude metal tail that causes it to dive and dart. The three treble hooks are held in place with cotter pins driven straight up through the body and then pounded over as an inexpert carpenter pounds over nails in a board. A few metallic sparkles are glued to the sides of the body. Old Sting is the plug a 9-year-old would build if you gave him wood, hooks, a tin can, and a hammer.

Old Sting

"Old Sting has taken more fish over 30 pounds than any other bait I have," says Pursch. "I don't like new baits. The worse they look, the better they are."

Pursch, a tall, lanky type with boyish blonde hair and sandy mustache, has been chasing muskies for a quarter century. During that time, he's developed a highly successful method of catching the big ones.

His methods aren't that unusual — he works spinners, crankbaits, and his favorite, big jerkbaits, over good structure, usually no more than about 20 feet deep. But he's found that a slower-than-normal retrieve produces more big muskies.

Pursch acknowledges that ripping a spinner through water as fast as you can has its place: it's especially

Don Pursch

Home: *Walker, Minnesota*

Occupation: *Muskie fishing guide*

Don Pursch has been a muskie fan since boyhood, when he spent his summers at the family cabin near Longville, in the heart of northern Minnesota's muskie country. Since then, he's earned a reputation for catching big fish. He has guided muskie anglers all over northern Minnesota, and is part-owner of Nielsen's Fly-In Camp on Rowan Lake in Ontario, where he leads clients to lake trout, largemouth bass, walleyes, and huge muskies.

In the past two years, Pursch has boated eleven muskies larger than 30 pounds. He's convinced there's a world-record muskie in Rowan. His biggest had a 55½-inch length and a 28½-inch girth. "I'm saying

conservatively 45 pounds. People say I was crazy letting a fish like that go."

"Fishing for a living has been a goal of mine all my life," Pursch says. For a while it was a goal he merely dreamed of from the confines of a custom rod-building shop; he fished only in his spare time. "It really happened when I left the rod shop and started with Camp Fish." For seven years he was the instructional director at the camp, a retreat near Walker where kids go to learn how to fish.

"During my days off I was guiding," he says. His later involvement with the In-Fisherman magazine and television shows "opened a lot of doors." He's appeared on many other shows as well, demonstrating his muskie techniques to nationally known TV anglers. He also conducts many seminars at outdoor sports shows.

Pursch excels in his sport by knowing his water and tailoring his methods to large fish. "I'm not looking for a 13- to 20-pound fish. I'm looking for big muskies. I want to catch the biggest ones."

good for catching lots of muskies. "It's fun to catch a muskie — any kind of muskie. But I'm interested in the big ones. I can fish for days and days and days to catch one of them. I want to learn about big fish and where they live. Even though they're the same species, the big fish don't do the same things the little guys do.

"These big fish are a lot like you and me. When we were younger, we could work all day, party all night, and still get to work on time. Now we come home, take our shoes off, grab some pop or cake out of the fridge, then sit down and relax. Big muskies want an easy meal. But 10-pounders are like little kids; they'll chase something all day."

The first step to catching big muskies is to fish big-muskie water. Today, a cool, sunny day in mid-October, we set out on Leech Lake in northern Minnesota. Vast and windswept, Leech is perhaps the best known of Minnesota's legendary muskie lakes. Ecologically, it is known as a "hard-water walleye lake," and besides muskies and walleyes,

Casting for muskies on a misty October morning

it harbors big pike, largemouth bass, and giant crappies. It also supports ample crops of yellow perch and ciscoes, the muskie's chief foods. Leech is filled with reefs, points, rocky shorelines, and abrupt dropoffs. The bottom is primarily sand and gravel.

In Leech, as in many big lakes, the muskies spawn in shallow bays in June and often are found around the first emerging weeds. "You can catch lots of small muskies, mostly males, in early season," Pursch observes. "My favorite early-season baits are minnow plugs and no. 5 Mepps spinners."

Rocky, windswept shores are prime muskie spots in fall

But as summer progresses, the muskies move to deep cabbage beds, rocky points, mid-lake rock reefs, and sharp dropoffs between a flat and much deeper water. "The big muskies start to bite about the third or fourth week of July," Pursch says, "and you can catch them through fall.

"The biggest muskies are probably in 25 to 30 feet of water, but I rarely fish that deep. If I'm fishing by myself, I may try trolling in deep water, But I'd much rather catch 'em on jerkbaits or spinners in shallower water so I can see the follows."

In August and September, large muskies move onto steep, rocky shores. "If you can find good green weeds yet, that's the most likely spot," Pursch contends. "You can catch muskies right up until the ice freezes. I've backed my trailer out over the ice until it cracked through. You get into that cold-weather period, and they're really putting on the beef. They'll take bigger lures than they will in summer — I've seen 'em swallow 5- to 7-pound fish this time of year."

On this particular day, we launch Pursch's boat and cross a large bay to just such a steep, rocky shore, pounded by an incoming wind. "Late in the year, the ciscoes move in here to spawn," Pursch says, "and the muskies and big pike move in with them. You can find cisco spawning areas by going out at night and shining the shoreline with a Q-Beam."

The waves are piling into the beach, tossing the boat. He shouts above the wind. "This is the kind of weather when I've had my best luck on this lake — you can barely stand up, you're taking on water, and catching 'em."

Pursch throws the motor into reverse at a slow trolling speed and, standing on the back seat, maneuvers the tiller with his foot to move us upwind, parallel to shore. We begin casting in, our lures splatting down in 6 to 10 feet of water. At times, according to the depth finder, the boat drifts over water more than 50 feet deep.

He sails Old Sting toward shore with a two-handed cast and immediately begins his retrieve. Tucking the handle under his left arm and grabbing the foregrip with his left hand for greater hook-setting power, he points the rod tip down to the water and

Retrieve jerkbait by holding rod as shown and jerking down

jerks the bait about a foot at a time. The rhythm is fairly steady, a bit more than a jerk a second, but he mixes in some faster or harder jerks to give the bait an erratic action. Between each jerk, he reels in line and then pauses to let the bait rise a bit. He also changes the bait's action by varying the amount of line reeled up between jerks.

It's important to keep the line taut during the entire retrieve. "If you get slack in your line, you won't

feel the strike. Be ready all the time. The first hook-set is always the best one. Slam him right away."

As Old Sting approaches the boat, he darts and rises, darts and rises. He swims no deeper than about 4 feet. "They'll come up to get him," Pursch says. "Big muskies will come up 15 feet. 'Easy meal,' they think. 'I can just go up and grab that.' "

Every so often, Pursch turns and launches a cast ahead of the boat, parallel to shore or at a slight angle to shore. "Whenever you can cast parallel to a break, you keep your bait in fish-holding water longer."

Pursch's tackle is built around the special demands of casting heavy jerkbaits and setting the hooks. Here's a rundown, from Old Sting upward to Pursch's right hand:

- Heavy-duty all-wire snap, 11-inch homemade leader fashioned from piano wire, and a ball-bearing swivel.

- More than 150 yards of 36-pound-test Dacron line, which has "zero stretch." The line is attached to the leader with a double-clinch knot (use five to six wraps).

- A 5-foot 9-inch long-handled graphite rod as stiff as a fireplace poker. Muskies, and big pike for that matter, sink their teeth into the soft wood of a jerkbait, making it awfully hard to move the lure and set the hooks. "Soft rods may be all right for 12- to 20-pound fish, but there's no way you're going to set the hook on a 30- to 40-pound fish," Pursch says.

- Large-capacity baitcasting reel. The star drag is cranked down tight for the hook-set, then backed off slightly during the fight.

As for the lures themselves, the Suick is one of Pursch's favorites, especially the 8-inch size (like

Pursch's favorite muskie lures

Old Sting), but he also uses the 10-inch model. He tunes the lures by pushing the metal fin on the rear downward and bending in the corners (photo below) to make the plug dive deeper. He also wraps short lengths of solder around the shafts of the trebles to leave the lure only slightly buoyant. "When that bait stops in front of them in mid-retrieve, *bang*, they hit it." Another jerkbait Pursch likes is the 8-inch Wade's Wobbler.

"Brown is very good," he says, and it's the most common color in Pursch's pile of jerkbaits. In discolored water, he prefers bright or fluorescent jerkbaits, especially yellow.

After several minutes and no strikes, Pursch lays down Old Sting and picks up a different rod with a Mepps bucktail spinner, his favorite bucktail. "More important than color is, number one, presentation, and number two, the size and shape of the bucktail you're throwing. I spend a lot of time underwater listening to spinner blades. It stands to reason that the high-pitched flutter of the willow-leaf blade sounds like a smaller food source. A big, round blade gives off a solid *whump, whump* and sounds like something bigger."

For the bucktails he uses a softer, longer rod, about 6½ feet. He reasons that the bucktails are a bit lighter than jerks, and also that muskies can't chomp down on them as tightly to interfere with the hook-set.

"There's one," Pursch utters excitedly, gesturing at a dark shadow with it's nose locked to the bucktail. But the fish turns away 10 feet from the boat. "If he had come a little closer, I'd have tried the figure eight."

Muskies are notorious for their habit of following a lure to the boat, but not striking. Pursch is widely known for his ability to take muskies at boatside with the figure-eight technique. To demonstrate, he makes a cast, then reels the spinner up to the boat. Pushing his rod into the water, he winds the end of the leader to the rod tip, thumbs the spool of his reel, and punches the free-spool button. He sticks the last 3 to 4 feet of the rod nearly straight down into the water and immediately sweeps it sideways, parallel to the side of the boat. Then he reverses direction, describing a figure-eight measuring about 6 feet from end to end.

"A big fish can't turn as quick as a small one, so make that figure-eight as big as you can reach. Then, when the fish is following, bring the bait back over his nose. Often, that's when he'll grab it. Don't worry about moving it too fast. If a

How Pursch Doctors Jerkbaits

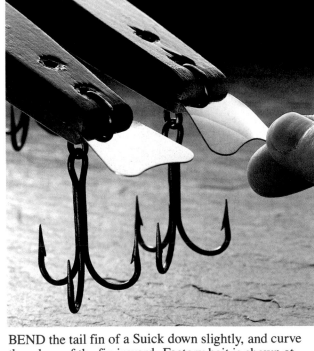

BEND the tail fin of a Suick down slightly, and curve the edges of the fin inward. Factory bait is shown at left, doctored bait at right. The altered fin makes the plug dive more steeply.

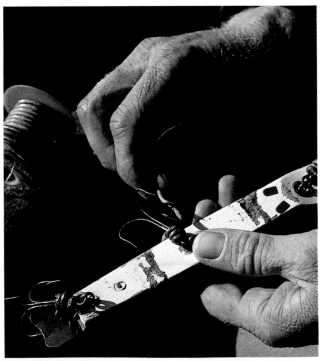

WRAP solder around shanks of treble hooks to decrease the lure's buoyancy. The extra weight keeps the lure down and allows a slower retrieve. Do not wrap the lower part of shank; the solder could interfere with hooking.

muskie wants it, he'll get it. Make sure your reel is in free spool. That way you can thumb it when he takes off.

"Once I figure-eighted a fish for at least five minutes until I was exhausted and quit. It just kept following the bait. Another time, two of us were figure-eighting fish in the front and back of the boat at the same time." Pursch recommends the figure eight whenever a fish follows, or when light or water conditions prevent you from seeing if indeed a muskie is behind your lure. It doesn't work all the time, but it's certainly worth a try.

Minutes later, Pursch proved just how effective the figure-eight technique can be. "There's another one," he whispered as he was about to lift his bucktail from the water. Instead, he plunged the rod into the lake and started making big figure eights. The fish stuck with the spinner for at least three complete figure eights, then suddenly the lure disappeared. "Got him," Pursch grunted as he set the hook. As if spring-loaded, the muskie came straight out of the water, then dove, sizzling off 20 yards of line. "Not a bad fish," Pursch remarked, calmly working it back to the boat.

He proceeded to demonstrate what he calls "the Leech Lake lip-lock." He led the tired fish alongside the boat, then grabbed it around the tail with one hand. He punched the reel into free spool, laid down the rod, slipped his fingers beneath the gill cover, and clamped his thumb alongside the lower jaw. He released the tail and freed the hooks with a pliers. The fish rested motionless for a few seconds, then with a flick of its tail darted away. "A good 42 inches," he estimated. "Chunky fish, maybe 20 pounds.

"A muskie fights hard and fast. Once it's tired, it becomes very docile. You can handle it in the water and release it unharmed."

To release muskies properly, Pursch suggests anglers carry a heavy-duty jaw spreader, long-handled needlenose pliers to remove hooks, and good side-cutters to cut off hooks buried deeply in the fish. A net is the surest way for a beginner to land a fish, but Pursch advises against it. "If you put a fish in a net, you may as well kill it. Ideally, you should never take a fish out of the water."

After the rocky shoreline produces several more follows but no strikes, Pursch motors to another of his favorite spots, a cabbage bed growing in about 14 feet of water. The weed tops rise within 5 feet of the surface. Like many cabbage beds in this lake, this one grows only on the break, so it's separated from the shore by a sand flat about 40 yards wide.

How to Figure-Eight a Muskie Following Your Lure

THUMB your spool when a muskie follows; quickly depress the free-spool button with your other thumb. Thumbing the spool will give precise control of line tension when you set the hook and the muskie makes a run.

PLUNGE your rod tip into the water and sweep your lure in a continuous figure-eight pattern. Bring the lure over the fish's nose; make the pattern large, about 6 feet across, so the fish will have space to turn and strike.

"Fish the deep side of the cabbage first," Pursch says. Only then should you move closer and fish over the cabbage. The fish's location seems to depend on light. On bright days, the fish are more likely to lie deep along the weedline. When the water is choppy or the day is cloudy, the fish will hang at the weed tops or roam the outside edge — and they will be more likely to strike.

It was at just this spot two years ago that Pursch caught his biggest Leech Lake muskie. "I pulled up to the weedbed and made a cast with Old Sting. I jerked only four or five times, and she hit. Her head came out of the water and shook four or five times, so I got a good look at her. Then she came right by the back of the boat and headed for deep water. They don't move fast, but they move with lots of power." After the fish circled the boat twice, Pursch hand-landed it. The fish measured 52 inches, which converts to about 40 pounds.

When the muskies refuse to hit spinners or jerk-baits, Pursch sometimes resorts to big crankbaits. A favorite is a gnarled jointed Pikie Minnow about 8 inches long with barely a shred of paint. Though Pikies are now made of plastic, Pursch says "the old ones — the best ones — are made out of cedar." Another good pick is a big-lipped Cisco Kid. He retrieves crankbaits much like jerkbaits — pull, reel, pull, reel. But the pulls are not as sharp as those used with a jerkbait.

Much of Pursch's success in catching big muskies is due to persistence. "I spend enough time on these lakes to know which spots are likely to hold big fish," he explains. "Just because I don't see a fish right away, I don't give up. I'll go back there again in an hour or two. Sometimes you have to work a spot over and over again before you get a big one to hit.

"You've also got to do some homework. I spend a lot of time talking to fishermen, guides, fisheries biologists and bait shop operators. I ask where they've been seeing muskies, whether the fish are active or not, and what the fish have been eating. This type of information will help you plan your fishing strategy.

"You also have to pay attention to the little things. Keep your hooks needle-sharp, check your knots often, and make sure your drag is set right. That way when you get your chance, you won't blow it."

How to Properly Release a Muskie

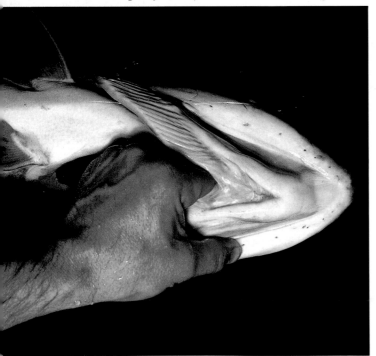

GRIP a played-out muskie with the "Leech Lake lip-lock," sliding your fingers under the gill cover and pressing against the jaw with your thumb. With this grip, the muskie normally stays docile, so you can easily unhook it.

HANDLE a muskie no more than necessary if you plan to release it. Often, you can leave the fish in the water while you grab the hook with a pliers and shake it loose. Hold the fish upright until it recovers and swims off.

Muskie & Northern Pike Tips

Paul Gasbarino
Downrigger Trolling for Suspended Fish

In many large northern lakes, pike and muskies suspend over deep water from summer through late fall to follow schools of ciscoes and whitefish. These scattered lunkers are tough to locate, but Paul Gasbarino finds them by trolling with downriggers. Gasbarino, a resident of Toronto and president of Muskies Canada, does most of his downrigger trolling in Georgian Bay of Lake Huron. He looks for deep saddles between islands, deep channels in the lake bottom leading from river mouths, and steep breaklines near windswept shallows. His favorite lures are big Pikie Minnows and Rapalas, Believers, spoons, and homemade plugs up to 14 inches long. He sets these 7 to 12 feet behind the downrigger balls, using 20-pound mono and 70-pound steel leaders 3 to 4 feet long.

Once he's on a spot with the right kind of structure, Gasbarino uses his graph to search out forage

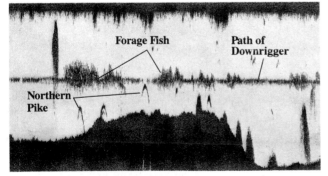

schools. In summer, he usually finds the forage at depths of 30 to 50 feet; in fall, 10 to 20 feet. He sets his downriggers accordingly.

Using this method, Gasbarino and other members of Muskies Canada consistently catch pike in the 20- to 30-pound range and have taken muskies up to 40 pounds.

Rich Vestecka
Slip-Bobber Rig for Weed Trolling

Bobber fishing for muskies and pike in the weeds can be a slow business — just sitting in one place and waiting for a feeder to come your way. In the experience of Rich Vestecka of Lincoln, Nebraska, a tournament pike and muskie angler, it's far more productive to take your bait to the fish. Hook a 6- to 12-inch sucker through the upper lip only, and troll it 6 to 8 feet below a slip-bobber. Work slowly along the edges of cabbage or coontail beds, then ease the rig right through the weeds, guiding it along channels and into pockets.

THREAD a cylinder float onto 20- to 35-pound braided line, then attach a bobber stop. Add a ⅝- to ¾-ounce bullet sinker and a bead. Next, tie on a snap-swivel, and crimp on a braided steel leader 18 to 24 inches long. To the leader, crimp on a Tru-Turn Stump Puller 125 weedless hook, size 7/0.

William Kellogg
Long-Hair Jigs

The size and action of an extra-long jig make it more appealing to pike than shorter ones. William Kellogg, co-owner of Bill and Jack's Marina at Fisher's Landing, New York, ties his own jigs with hair tails 6 to 8 inches long. He fishes them by casting or vertical jigging near points and islands in the St. Lawrence River. It's best to work them just above rocky bottoms, he reports, at depths of 25 to 30 feet.

Kellogg's pike jigs (inset) have ½- to ¾-ounce banana heads or keel heads; the tails are tied with horsehair, dyed nylon, or hair from a wig.

Muskie Tips from Ron Kobes

Tinsel-Tail Jerkbaits

In muskie angling, one of the most frustrating — though exciting — occurrences comes when a good fish follows the lure but refuses to take. The fish will dog your offering almost to the rod tip, then swerve away at the last moment. Ron Kobes decks out his jerkbaits with a tinsel skirt, adding flash that can excite these followers into striking. The metallic tinsel is available at hobby shops.

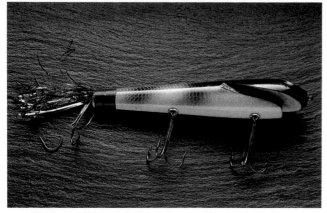

FASTEN 4-inch strands of tinsel to the rear of a jerkbait, on the sides and top only, using electrical tape. Snip off the top prong of the rear treble, so the skirt won't foul on it.

Twister-Tail Trailer

Another way to provoke muskie strikes, according to Ron Kobes, is to rig a twister-tail trailer well back from the lure. The fish often go for the twister tail at the rear when they won't hit the bigger bait up front that first drew their attention. The lures Kobes likes to rig this way are bucktail spinners and tail-finned jerkbaits such as Bobbies and Suicks. This tip doesn't work with wobbling plugs, since the long wire running back to the trailer will ruin their side-to-side action.

ATTACH a size 1 salmon-egg hook to a 12- to 14-inch length of 124-pound stainless wire. Twist wire around shank so hook is rigid; thread on twister tail. Connect wire to bucktail by twisting it around shank of rear treble; to jerkbait by threading it down hole in fin, then twisting it onto rear hook hanger.

RON KOBES guides for muskies and pike in northern Minnesota. In a three-year period, Kobes had one first-place finish and two second-place finishes in the International World Northern Pike Tournament.

Reversed Teddie Bait

When the water is cold or muddy, a jerkbait fished with a slow retrieve catches more pike and muskies than one fished with the usual rapid, jerking motion. But a standard jerkbait won't dive much when fished slowly, so Ron Kobes reverses a Teddie bait, so it runs tailfirst. This way, the bait tracks several feet deeper with a wider side-to-side action.

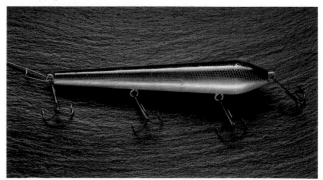

OPEN the front screw eye, then attach a treble hook. Fasten your wire leader to the eye at the other end, leaving the hook in place.

Panfish

Icing Jumbo Perch

by Dick Sternberg

Rod Sather divulges the jigging technique that has accounted for hundreds of 2-pound perch

R od Sather may be the only guide in the country who's disappointed when he lands a pound-and-a-half walleye. "Rather eat perch," he says. "Firmer meat and better tasting." His philosophy is easy to understand: the yellow perch he catches through the ice are often bigger than walleyes.

Before you can catch jumbo perch, you have to select a lake that's got them, preferably in good numbers. Sather does his guiding on Devils Lake in North Dakota, which he considers the top perch lake on the continent.

Devils Lake, like most good perch lakes, is big — 65,000 acres, to be exact. The maximum depth is 28 feet, so all the acreage is usable perch habitat. Interestingly, Devils Lake was almost dry during the drought of the 1930s, and there were no fish in the lake until the early 1960s.

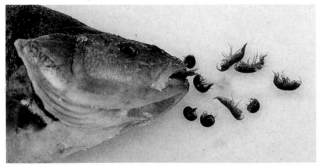

Yellow perch and prime forage: freshwater shrimp

Rod explains that the lake water is highly alkaline: that is, the content of salts and other minerals is great. The unusually fertile water supports a

tremendous crop of freshwater shrimp, which make ideal forage for the perch and account for their large size.

The largest perch ever caught from Devils Lake weighed 2 pounds 15½ ounces and was taken in 1982. This fish is also the official North Dakota record. However, Rod knows of several 3-pounders caught with test nets in Devils Lake, so he expects the record to topple soon.

Although Rod prefers Devils Lake, he's fished for perch in other alkaline lakes throughout the Dakotas. His top picks in North Dakota include Gackle Slough, Coal Mine Lake, and Lake

---

Rod Sather

Home: *Devils Lake, North Dakota*

Occupation: *Fishing and hunting guide; manager of Towers Bait And Tackle Shop near Devils Lake*

If you walked into Ed's Bait Shop in Devils Lake, North Dakota, you'd be stunned by a wall display of thirteen mounted perch, each weighing 2 pounds or better. At first glance, they don't even look like perch. Their backs are more steeply humped than those of normal yellow perch, and their bodies look about twice as deep. But the most amazing thing about these fish is that all were caught by a single angler — a relentless perch-hound named Rod Sather.

Sather is a modest man, not prone to bragging about his fishing accomplishments. It takes plenty of prodding to get him to reveal his catch statistics. On a typical day of ice fishing, Rod and his customers will catch a hundred perch, half of them running from 1 to 2½ pounds. Through an average winter, they'll catch more than a hundred fish weighing 2 pounds or heavier. Sather's biggest single perch went 2 pounds 9 ounces.

Rod also fishes for other species, often in tournaments. In fact, he's taken first-place honors in 25 different tournaments; in one recent competition, for northern pike, walleyes, and nongame species, his total catch weighed twice as much as the runner-up's.

Sather likes to fish perch in morning and late afternoon

Ashtabula. In South Dakota, he says, try Roy Lake, Lake Poinsett, and Lake Andes. He also recommends Mille Lacs Lake in Minnesota, although the perch there are not as big, topping off at about 1½ pounds.

Rod does most of his perch fishing in winter. The perch seem to bite best then, probably because food is scarcer than in summer and the water is much clearer, making the bait easier to see. And during the winter, female perch, which are considerably larger than males, dominate the catch. The females bite better in winter because their bodies need an ample supply of fat to nourish the developing eggs.

Early ice is best; in most years, the ice is thick enough to walk on by December 1. Rod does most of his early fishing on Creel Bay, because it's sheltered from the wind and freezes up earlier than the rest of the lake. Peak early-ice fishing continues until just before Christmas.

The perch continue to bite through the winter, but the action is not as consistent. There are good days and bad ones, depending on the weather and moon phase. Rod prefers a partly cloudy day a few days on either side of the full moon or new moon. The fishing usually slows right after a cold front, but after a few days of cold weather, the perch start to bite again.

Prime Ice-Fishing Spots on Devils Lake

Early-winter spots are usually in protected areas that freeze up first. Midwinter spots have extensive weedy flats extending from shore and dropping into deep water. Late-winter spots are near spawning areas and may be very shallow, sometimes only 3 feet deep. The best wintertime spots are generally next to moving water or springs.

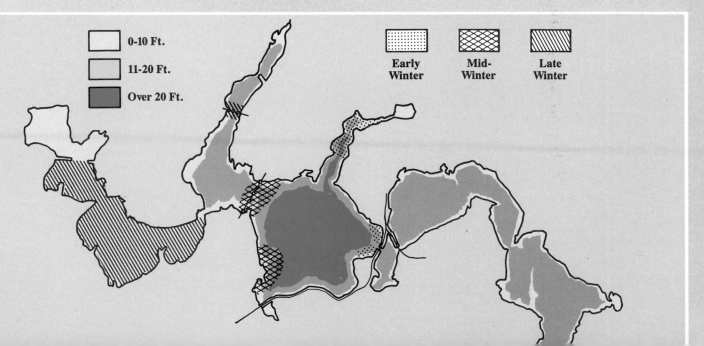

0-10 Ft.

11-20 Ft.

Over 20 Ft.

Early Winter

Mid-Winter

Late Winter

The action picks up in late winter, starting around March 1 and continuing until the season closes on March 20 or thereabouts. Even after March 20, perch fishing is still permitted on parts of Devils Lake, and the action is fast until ice-out around April 15. Late winter offers not only the biggest perch, but also the warmest weather.

Rod likes to fish in midweek, Tuesday through Thursday, when fishing pressure is lightest. He recommends staying away from crowds because the sound of power augers drives the perch away, especially in shallow water. If you locate a school of perch and have it to yourself, you can often enjoy good fishing for hours before the fish move.

You'll normally find Rod on the lake before sunrise. He believes the perch bite best from sunrise until noon, then again from 3 p.m. until dark. But when they're really biting, you can catch them all day long. Night fishing is usually poor.

His favorite technique for locating jumbo perch is to find a weedbed, then fish just out from the weedline. In Devils Lake, submerged weeds grow to a depth of 9 feet, so Rod normally starts fishing at about 10 feet.

Not all the perch are that shallow, however. Rod often finds deep schools and shallow ones at the same time. It's not unusual to find one active school at 10 feet, and another as deep as 28. On a trip the Hunting and Fishing Library staff made with Rod, we caught most of our big perch on a 16-foot midlake flat with no vegetation and no structure. We found the fish by drilling holes over a large area and fishing no longer than a few minutes in each one.

In early winter, Rod uses a Si-Tex color flasher for locating perch. If the ice is free of slush and no more than 6 inches thick, he pours a little water on it, then sounds through the ice rather than drilling holes. The perch show up as red or orange blips just off bottom.

As a general rule, Rod fishes deeper on sunny days than on cloudy ones. After a storm front passes, he often finds the perch right in the weeds, as shallow as 5 feet.

Anyone can catch small perch, but it takes more skill to catch the big ones consistently. Rod's advice: "If you're catching little perch, move. You may catch a big one mixed in with the little guys, but the big ones are usually by themselves. The only way to find them is to keep looking."

Another tip: "If you want to catch bigger perch, use bigger bait. I like a 1/8-ounce Limpet spoon with the treble hook loaded with spikes or waxworms. I put three spikes [maggots or silver wigglers] or a single waxworm on each prong of the treble." Larger baits work best, probably because a big perch would rather eat a minnow than a freshwater shrimp or other small food item. If you use a small bait — a teardrop with a single

Sather's Favorite Perch Baits and Lures

LURES AND BAITS for ice fishing include: (1) Kastmaster spoon baited with EuroLarvae, (2) Kastmaster spoon baited with perch eye, (3) Jigging Rapala® tipped with waxworm, (4) Jigging Rapala®, (5) Swedish Pimple® baited with perch eye, (6) mayfly nymph , (7) fathead minnow, (8) waxworms.

waxworm, for instance — you'll be pestered by little perch.

Besides the Limpet spoon, which is no longer being made, Rod uses a variety of baits and lures including:

• A ⅛-ounce blue-and-chrome Kastmaster spoon, with two or three spikes on a 4-inch dropper. EuroLarvae can be substituted for spikes. The small larvae evidently imitate freshwater shrimp.

• The same Kastmaster rig baited with a perch eye.

• A size 3 Jigging Rapala — in perch color for overcast days, chartreuse for bright days.

• A size 3 Jigging Rapala in orange and chartreuse, baited with a waxworm.

• A size 3 Swedish Pimple with a single hook instead of a treble, baited with a perch eye.

• A 2- to 2½-inch fathead minnow or a pair of 1½-inchers, hooked lightly just ahead of the dorsal fin with a size 8 hook and fished under a small slip-bobber.

When fishing is really tough, Rod uses an unusual bait: mayfly nymphs. The nymphs are difficult to get and must be imported from Wisconsin. They're soft-bodied and hard to keep on the hook, but when perch are fussy, the nymphs make a big difference. Another good bait for tough conditions is simply a waxworm or spike on a plain size 10 short-shank hook.

Rod's perch outfit consists of a 24-inch medium-action graphite rod; an ultralight open-face spinning reel; and limp 4-pound mono, either green or clear. Devils Lake has a good population of walleyes up to 11 pounds, and they hang out in the same areas as the perch, so he uses a reel with a good drag. To reduce icing problems, he puts an oversized tip guide on his rod.

Other equipment includes an 8-inch Jiffy power auger; a 5-gallon pail with an elevated seat, which also serves for storing the perch; a small plastic tackle box for lures; and a homemade sled designed to carry his gear. In early winter, he carries an 8-inch Strikemaster hand auger: it's quieter than a power auger and doesn't seem to spook the perch. In late winter, he normally uses an 8-inch extension on his power auger, because the ice may be 40 inches thick.

Instead of using a bobber, Rod prefers to jig, lowering the bait to the bottom, then lifting it. With a bobber, you can't lower the bait far enough. A bobber isn't necessary to detect bites; a graphite rod transmits any light tap. If the perch are biting soft, Rod attaches a spring bobber to his rod tip. He may use a slip-bobber on a second line, however.

Rod's advice on jigging: "Jig down instead of up. Perch always are close to the bottom, and if you jerk the bait up too far, they won't chase it. I lift the bait slowly until it's a few inches off bottom, then I lower it to bottom while twitching the rod. Lots of times they grab the bait right on bottom. When you start lifting the rod, you'll feel weight. That means set the hook.

"I always tell my customers to sharpen their hooks. They'll tell me they're already sharp, but usually they aren't, even if the lure is brand-new. A sharp hook can make the difference between a pail of jumbos or just a few stragglers."

Homemade sled carries all gear, has padded seat

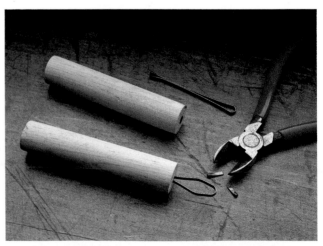

MAKE a perch-eye remover by drilling a small hole in a 1-inch dowel, then inserting a bobby pin with the ends snipped off. Spread the loop and sharpen the inside edges with a small file. Use the eyes to tip jigging lures.

How Sather Jigs for Jumbo Perch

LIFT the spoon slowly until it's about 10 inches off bottom. The spikes or waxworms will then be about 6 inches off bottom.

LOWER the spoon all the way to bottom, keeping the line taut and twitching the rod tip as the spoon is sinking.

SET THE HOOK if you feel a twitch, or if the line moves to the side. Sometimes perch will push the bait up, causing the line to slacken.

How Sather Cleans and Cooks Perch

In good perch country you measure your catch not in numbers of fish, but in numbers of 5-gallon pails. Many states, including North Dakota, set no limit on perch. That means you'll have a real cleaning chore when you get home.

If your perch are half-pounders or bigger, you'll probably want to fillet them. Rod makes short work of it by using an electric knife. The blades slice easily through the heavy rib bones, reducing cleaning time by as much as 50 percent. To save even more time, he cuts off the belly meat,

rather than trimming around it. He loses a little meat this way, but the remaining fillets are of uniform thickness, so they cook evenly.

The real payoff in perch fishing comes at the dinner table. Perch have firm, flaky meat, with a hint of sweetness. Rod's recipe is simple: dip the fillets in a batter such as Shorelunch, then deep-fry them at about 375°F until they're golden brown. Once you try fillets prepared this way, you'll be sharpening your perch hooks too.

World's Best Crappie Bait?

by Frank Sargeant

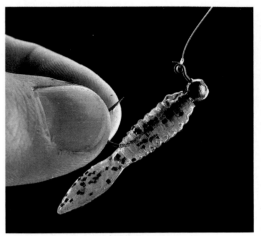

Tom Floroski catches plenty of giant crappies on his paddletail grubs, but …

> **Tom Floroski**
>
> **Home:** *Milford, Connecticut*
>
> **Occupation:** *Medical electronics technician*
>
> ---
>
> *Tom Floroski grew up in Connecticut and spent a good share of his youth fishing for panfish and bass. He still pursues those species with a passion. In the early 1980s, Floroski started fishing in bass tournaments at the urging of Russ Hall, winning the first two tournaments he entered. But he especially likes fishing for crappies. "I love crappies of any size," he says, "and catching the big ones is as much a challenge as catching a 10-pound bass." On a recent trip, Floroski boated several crappies over 2 pounds and a pair over 3 pounds, the biggest weighing in at 3 pounds 4 ounces.*

Tom Floroski and Russ Hall are alike in a lot of ways. Both of the bearded giants are prominent names in Connecticut fishing. Between them, they've won the state tournament bass championships ten times running.

Both started fishing at age 5. And both enjoy catching crappies as much as bass. Their specialty is slab crappies, 2- to 3-pounders. They fish together much of the time, and a good deal of their tournament fishing is done as a team. Aside from that, they get out two or three times a week for fun, spring through fall; and in the winter they team up on a few ice-fishing trips.

They even operate the same type of boat, a vintage Ranger, and they

… Russ Hall, his fishing partner, says that kellies are the world's best crappie bait

use many of the same angling techniques. But when it comes to crappie fishing, they go about things a little differently.

Floroski prefers to fish fast and cover a lot of water, so he relies heavily on small jigs tipped with plastic grub bodies. His favorite design is a simple paddletail — no wriggling tail or octopus legs to help attract attention. "I can locate the fish with jigs a lot faster than with minnows," he explains.

Hall's philosophy: "Nothing imitates live bait like live bait." Most of the time, he knows where the fish are, so it's just a matter of giving them a bait that they like. And, according to Hall, "The world's best live bait for crappies is kellies."

Russ Hall

Home: *Orange, Connecticut*

Occupation: *Inspector at aircraft-engine plant*

Russ Hall is the founder of a bass-fishing club in Connecticut, but like Tom Floroski, he'd just as soon fish for crappies. "I love the competition of bass tournaments," he says, "but when I fish for fun and food I'd rather have crappies." Hall takes his fishing seriously, logging the results of every trip, then studying the log carefully to help plan future trips. "A person has to pay his dues and invest a lot of time to become a good fisherman," he says. "When I was growing up, I didn't chase girls or get into trouble — I was too busy fishing."

Hall (foreground) and Floroski get started early

When Hall refers to kellies, he actually means mummichogs, which are members of the killifish family. Mummichogs are extremely hardy baitfish found mainly in brackish waters along the Atlantic coast, particularly in estuaries and salt marshes. Presumably, the name "kelly" is a shortened version of the family name.

Both anglers admit that they'll switch to different baits when their favorites aren't working. Floroski always keeps a few kellies handy, just in case. "What usually happens is you get on the fish with a jig, and you catch four or five, then they seem to get wise to it," he says. "When that happens, you either have to back off the spot and rest it thirty minutes or so, or you have to switch to live bait. I'd rather switch. When you do, you can usually go ahead and catch all you want, as long as you stay well back from the spot and don't run your trolling motor right on top of them." Similarly, Hall may use a jig when he's prospecting new water.

Recently, I joined the pair for a few days of fishing, so I had a chance to observe their crappie-catching tactics firsthand.

I'd timed my trip just about right. It was late October, and the very best period for lunker crappies, they say, is fall and early winter.

"Crappies are scattered all over a lake or river in summer," Hall explains, "but when the water drops below 50 degrees, they start to school up and feed really strong wherever they can find baitfish concentrations. In the lakes around here, that's usually over offshore humps, water maybe 5 or 6 feet deep next to drops into maybe 20 or 30 feet.

"In the Connecticut River, they move into the boat basins and marinas — again, about the same depth, with plenty of little baitfish hanging around the docks and underwater cover."

The days I was with them, we fished the river, probing a boat basin that covered about two acres. While yachtsmen rushed to pull out their boats ahead of the freeze-up, we eased around the docks in the team's Ranger bass boats and just about wore ourselves out catching fish.

On the first day, I went with Floroski. We fished mainly with 1/32-ounce jig heads rigged with 1/2-inch paddletail grubs in a silver-smoke shade. The tiny lures are tossed up against docks, pilings or other cover.

The trick with either jigs or live bait is to get the offering very close to the spot where the crappies are holding. In the marinas, you have to cast right up to the docks, so the jig or bait falls within an inch or two of the cover.

Floroski's favorite jigs: (1-4) Cabela's Pro Crappie Jigs; (5-6) Toledo Tackle's Feather Grubs

"The fish don't want to move much in the cold water," Floroski says. "If you toss it a foot away from the spot where they're at, you won't get half as many hits."

After you cast the jig, you allow it to sink all the way to bottom, then you retrieve it in minute twitches. That is, you *try* to retrieve it in minute twitches. More than half the time, something would eat the jig before we could start to crank. Sometimes it was a slab crappie. And if a crappie didn't take the jig, a yellow perch, bluegill, or junior-sized largemouth did. The basin was stiff with panfish of all types.

Floroski notes that a deft touch is necessary when fishing the small jigs. For maximum sensitivity he recommends a 5-foot light graphite spinning rod, an ultralight spinning reel, and 4- or 6-pound mono. "The fish don't want much motion in the lure. Sometimes a fish just eats it and the only way you know it's there is by feeling resistance, so I set

the hook whenever anything feels the slightest bit unusual. A lot of times when the lure is dropping, you won't feel anything at all. But you might see the line twitch just a bit, the way it will when a bass takes a sinking plastic worm."

Floroski's strategy paid off — during the course of the afternoon, we caught well over a hundred panfish, including several pound-and-a-half crappies.

The next morning, Hall and I went back to the same spot, this time toting a bucket full of kellies.

"When it's cold, kellies will live in wet moss," Hall says. "You don't even have to keep them in water. They're easy to catch, too. You can seine them, or trap them. Put a can of cat food in a wire trap and set it in shallow water in a tidal creek. Next morning, the trap will be stuffed with them. You don't have to aerate the water to keep them alive. They stay calm in the bait bucket so they're not killing themselves by banging the sides like

How to Catch and Keep Kellies

TRAP kellies by placing a wire minnow trap in shallow, brackish water in a tidal creek or salt marsh. Bait the trap with a can of cat food.

KEEP the kellies alive in cold weather in a container filled with damp grass or moss. In warmer weather, keep them in water in a bait bucket.

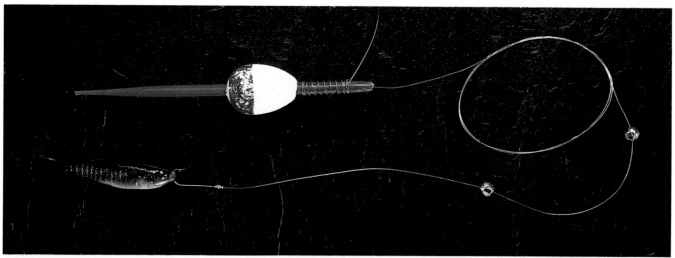

Hall's crappie rig baited with a kelly

Crappies hang near marina dock posts in late fall

shiners do. And they're tough — you can catch two crappies on one bait if you want to."

A little while after he told me this, he managed to catch four crappies on a single 2-inch kelly. When he finally took it off the hook, it still had the grit to swim slowly off.

Hall fishes his kellies on light-wire hooks, size 4 or 6, running the sharpened points through the thin membrane just behind their lips. He uses a spring-lock bobber with a body about the size of a dime and a 3-inch quill. He adds two or three split-shot so the body of the float sinks, leaving only the quill

above water. When a crappie takes, the quill drops like a periscope below the surface — or on occasion, pops to the surface and lies on its side.

"Crappies sometimes take from below, rising up to gulp the bait," Hall says. "When that happens, the bobber flops over instead of dropping, because they're raising the sinkers right up with the bait. That's the time to set the hook."

Hall's tackle includes a 6-foot graphite spinning rod, light power, and a spinning reel spooled with 4- or 6-pound mono. The outfit is not as sensitive as Floroski's ultralight, but sensitivity is not much

Hall reels in crappie that hit within inches of dock

of an issue when bobber-fishing, and the longer rod works better for setting the hook.

In just over two hours, Hall and I iced maybe fifty whopper crappies, with a few pushing 2 pounds. We caught considerably fewer small panfish than Floroski and I had taken the previous day, but the difference may have been due in part to a change in the weather. A cold front passed through overnight, and Hall speculated that the chilly weather may have moved the big crappies into the boat basin.

But even if the weather played a role in our success, it's difficult to deny that kellies are a tremendous crappie bait.

It's surprising that a bait so effective hasn't gained popularity in other regions of the country. Although kellies are found only along the coast, other species of killifish are widely distributed and would probably work nearly as well. The banded killifish, for instance, is found throughout the northeastern and north-central states, as far west as the Dakotas.

During my short stay, we did all of our fishing in Connecticut River boat basins and marinas. We didn't have a chance to fish the team's other prime fall and early-winter spots — submerged humps in area lakes. Nevertheless, the team offered some advice on fishing spots of this type. First, they find the right kind of hump using a chart recorder or flasher. If they spot fish, they mark the hump with a plastic float. After that, they back off to sieve it with casts until they home in on a school of crappies.

Once they have a school pinpointed, both anglers prefer to anchor upwind at the edge of casting range, rather than continue drifting or controlling the boat with the electric motor. "The more the boat moves around, the sooner the fish stop biting," Hall says.

Though some anglers contend that crappies and most other fish slow down their feeding as colder weather arrives, Hall and Floroski believe otherwise. "We've had good fishing right into December most years," Hall notes. "In fact, on the days we've caught the largest crappies of the year, we've actually had to use the boats as icebreakers in the marinas, running them up on the ice and cracking the skin. Then we go somewhere else and do the same thing, and half an hour later come back to the first spot and catch big fish."

The ice sets in permanently sometime in late December or early January, depending on whether the power plant up the river is heating the water. Even after ice-up, Floroski says, crappies will continue to bite for those hardy enough to go after them.

The bearded giants are definitely hardy enough.

Hall lands a "slab" that pushes 2 pounds

Turning the Worm on Sunfish

by Jake Barnes

George LaFrance uses his homegrown crawlers to catch record numbers of "citation" sunfish

I magine a 60-year-old grandfather crawling on hands and knees across his backyard, punching holes in the ground with a long-shank screwdriver. Aerating the grass, you say? Or stabbing moles? Wrong. He's making nightcrawler condos.

George LaFrance resorted to this madness for good reason. He knew that nightcrawlers were the best bait for the plate-sized sunfish he loved to catch. But crawlers don't normally live in southern Virginia, so he hauled some in from the northern part of the state. At first, he tried putting the crawlers on top of the ground, but they wouldn't dig down. So he got a big screwdriver and started poking holes — nightcrawler condos, so to speak. Then he carefully inserted the worms one by one. He covered the holes with dirt; the new residents took over from there, boring tunnels of their own. Today, the LaFrance neighborhood crawls with his worms.

This scenario illustrates LaFrance's unyielding commitment to perfection when it comes to catching sunfish. He'll do whatever it takes to boost his odds of bagging jumbo bluegills and shellcrackers.

George now does most of his fishing on Western Branch, a 1600-acre reservoir in the tidewater plains of Virginia. The reservoir, one of seven supplying the Norfolk sprawl, can be reached only by a labyrinth of back roads. Its launching ramp, and its tidy new bait and tackle shop, do not draw itinerant fishermen, just the local hardcore.

Besides keeping the taps running in Norfolk, Western Branch grows lots of fish. Bass, catfish, bluegills, redears, white perch, yellow perch, pickerel, northern pike, gar, carp, even stripers swim in what Norfolk drinks.

LaFrance believes it's best to concentrate on one or two lakes rather than jumping around to dozens.

George LaFrance

Home: *Hampton, Virginia*

Occupation: *Retired, after 20 years in the Air Force and 18 years in the Postal Service*

George LaFrance is a man blessed with an intuitive sense of how to catch fish — and also with the dedication, teetering on fanaticism, to stick with his intuition. When he was 3½ in Nashua, New Hampshire, he wandered down to the town pond alone and caught a stout pickerel with a bent pin and string. Since that tender age, he's been a diehard angler.

While in the Air Force, George caught Nile perch in the Philippines, trout in California, and bass in other

parts of the U.S. On retiring from the military in the mid-1960s, he began to concentrate on sunfish — both bluegills and redears (also known as shellcrackers). His expertise in catching big sunfish throughout the year in deep water has made him the column of choice for tidewater Virginia sportswriters: when nothing new is breaking, do a George LaFrance piece.

Virginia issues citations of achievement for catching big fish. For sunfish, the minimum weight for recognition is 1 pound. George has more than 200 citations for sunfish, as well as citations for ten other species. His biggest sunfish is an eye-popping 2½-pound bluegill, from Folsom Lake in California.

Today LaFrance is less interested in winning awards than in simply having fun on the water. He puts in 300 days fishing a year, often in the company of one of his five grandchildren — each of whom, not surprisingly, has taken a citation fish while out with granddad.

Gathering worms at night; LaFrance often uses a flashlight covered with red cellophane to avoid spooking them

He says he plans to study Western Branch "until I know every inch of it, until I know what the fish are doing on any day, in any weather."

Although George catches good-sized bass, catfish, and even stripers in Western Branch, he specializes in sunfish. It doesn't matter what kind. Whichever species is biting is George's fixation for the day.

He pursues sunfish with as much intensity and attention to detail as any muskie or trout addict. But he doesn't believe in buying every new lure and electronic device; instead, he holds to tackle, bait, and techniques that he's mastered over many years.

LaFrance likes small, dull-colored boat

A day on the water with George LaFrance starts at sunup, when he launches his modest boat on Western Branch Reservoir. The boat is a 14-foot Sears Gamefisher, made of fiberglass and painted dark green. He believes a bright-colored or shiny boat will spook fish in shallow water. He also believes that even the slightest noise will spook them. To deaden sound, George refinished the interior of his boat with a product called Liquid Carpet, a paint texturized with particles of rubber.

There's a souped-up 9.9-horse Evinrude on the stern, and an electric trolling motor with a foot control and a Maximizer on the bow. The boat is equipped with a flasher, but no graph or liquid crystal recorder. LaFrance has nothing against high-tech electronics, he just doesn't need them. A swivel seat amidships places George within a spin of a small cooler, where he keeps sodas and worms; a larger cooler, where he stores his catch; and a couple of storage compartments for terminal tackle, towels, and the other junk all fisherman acquire. The boat may not attract many admirers, but it's highly functional.

George goes after sunfish year around. He has studied the fish so carefully that he can tell you exactly where to find them every month of the year.

He finds bluegills and shellcrackers in pretty much the same places, although there are some differences in early season. Shellcrackers are the first to move into the spawning areas. In April and May he finds them on 2- to 4-foot shoreline flats. He pinpoints these flats by looking for areas where the land slopes gently away from the water. Bluegills move in to spawn a little later than shellcrackers, usually in May and June.

The larger females leave the nesting area first; the smaller males stay behind to guard the nests. After leaving the nesting area, the fish move to sunken islands that top off at 8 or 9 feet, or to creek channels between the spawning area and the main river channel. The fish remain in these areas, generally at depths of 8 to 12 feet, through June and July.

By August, most of the fish have moved to the main river channel where the water is deepest and coolest. This is LaFrance's favorite time to fish, because the big sunfish are concentrated. They seek out stair-step ledges along the channel edge, areas where a shallow ridge or sunken island meet the channel, and junctions where creek channels and old roadbeds meet the main channel. The most productive late-summer depth is around 15 feet.

One reason sunfish are more concentrated in late summer is that the deep-water structure is more pronounced than the shallow-water structure. "In the shallows the old channel edges get eroded by waves and currents," LaFrance says, "but in deep water they stay sharp. So in that deep water I like to fish right where the channel drops off. I'll try to pick up the fish on my flasher first. Once I lock on to the depth where they're holding, I'll stick there all day."

As the water starts to cool in September, the fish move somewhat shallower, 8 to 12 feet, but they stay on the same structure where they were in late summer. As the water continues to cool, they gradually slip into deeper water along the river channel. By midwinter, they're at depths of 20 to 25 feet. They stay deep until the water starts warming in spring, then they follow the creek channels to their spawning grounds.

George's tackle and rigging are simple. One rod is a floppy glass fly rod, rebuilt as a spinning rig with Fuji guides and a cork spinning grip; the other is a very soft, very old spinning rod. Unlike the stiff graphite rods popular today, these won't snap a lightly impaled worm off the hook on a cast. His well-used spinning reels are spooled with 8-pound yellow fluorescent mono. That's heavy line for sunfish, certainly, but remember that sunfish aren't the only inhabitants of Western Branch. George likes to know he has guts in his line should a bigger fish suck down his worm.

The water in Western Branch is cloudy enough that the fluorescent line doesn't alert the fish, yet it gives him an advantage in detecting the lightest bites. George does not use a bobber; he simply watches the highly visible line.

He rigs the business end in an unorthodox manner. The hook is a size 1 or 1/0 gold Aberdeen. He says this large hook doesn't discourage the heavyweight sunfish he's after, and it holds more securely than a tiny hook should he hang into a big catfish or striper.

LaFrance ties his rig a special way so the hook stands out at a right angle to the line. With the hook tied this way, George feels his hooking percentage is higher than if the hook were hanging straight down. To make the hook stand out, he ties the line to one side of the hook eye, then ties a 12- to 18-inch dropper to the opposite side. A single split-shot crimped to the dropper puts just enough pull on the hook to keep it at a right angle. The

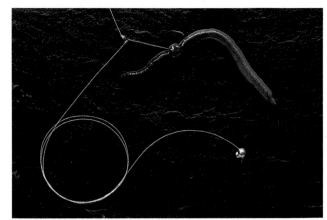

The special right-angle rig LaFrance prefers

split-shot rides along bottom with the bait above it. This way, the hook doesn't snag as often and the bait is more visible to the fish.

This is the rig George uses for practically all of his deep-water fishing. Only in water shallower than 6 feet does he omit the dropper and shot; there the hook and bait alone are heavy enough to get to the bottom.

Where LaFrance Finds Sunfish in Shallow Reservoirs

In spring, sunfish spawn on (A) flats from 2 to 4 feet deep. After spawning, they move to depths of 8 to 12 feet in (B) old creek channels and around (C) submerged points and islands. From late summer through winter, look for them at 15 to 25 feet, where the old river channel meets a (D) point or (E) old creek channel.

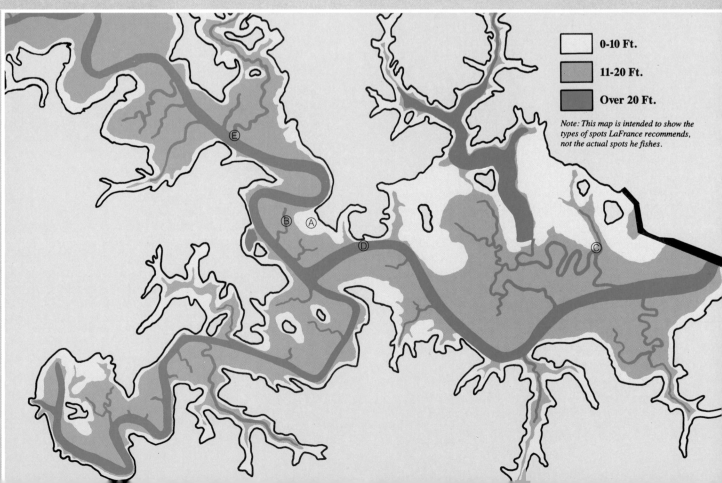

☐	**0-10 Ft.**
▨	**11-20 Ft.**
▓	**Over 20 Ft.**

Note: This map is intended to show the types of spots LaFrance recommends, not the actual spots he fishes.

Another citation redear, well over the 1-pound mark

When George approaches a piece of structure he wants to fish, he cuts the outboard, drops his electric and motors quietly into position. His usual plan is to start fishing shallow, then work progressively deeper until he hits big sunfish.

George rigs both rods alike. He drops one worm over the side, directly under the boat, then slides the rod handle under his thigh. He casts the other worm 30 feet out in a gentle arc so as not to flip it off the hook. He disengages the anti-reverse on the reel and ever so slowly retrieves the worm. By working the handle forward and then back, he can retrieve the worm in small increments and alternately place just a hint of slack in the line. When that slack twitches, a fish is on.

While gingerly working that rod, George continually jigs and fiddles with the other one clamped under his thigh. Concurrently, his eyes are locked on his flasher and he deftly controls the electric motor with his foot, holding the boat against a gentle breeze one moment, sliding closer to the structure the next, then moving sideways to another part of it.

At the slightest indication something might be wrong — weeds on his hook, or a messed-up worm — George reels in. If a small fish nibbles off some of the worm, he puts on a fresh one. He may pinch on an additional shot if the water is deep, or remove the shot and dropper if the water is shallow. He never stops thinking and adjusting his tactics.

LaFrance covers a given piece of water thoroughly in this manner. As he studies his flasher, he offers a blow-by-blow description of what's happening below: "Here come some weeds at 12 feet. Oh, look, now there's a fish. Perch probably, up that close. Now here's the channel. There're some bluegill, I bet, 18 feet." This monologue continues across every square foot of water. And most of the time, George's rods twitch out confirmation of his forecasts.

George may cover only 30 or 40 yards of channel edge in an hour. He moves his boat along very slowly, precisely following the contour while probing the channel with his worms. Sticking there is methodical, intense work. If someone were paid to fish this hard, from sunup till dusk, he'd call it grueling work.

"If a man loves what he's doing, though," says George, "it's art." The smile that never leaves his face from launch time until sunset widens. Out goes another worm. And in comes another 1-pound redear.

An artist is at work.

Nightcrawlers are his preferred bait for almost everything — even striped bass. For a day of fishing, he'll take along 200 of his homegrown worms. He generally uses a whole nightcrawler, inserting the hook in front of the collar and threading on an inch or so.

The rig, with or without the dropper, looks like something a child might devise. Most experts wouldn't even consider using heavy fluorescent line. They would argue that the hook is way too big for sunfish and far too obvious to deceive any fish at all. They would say that sunfish would nibble off the lightly hooked worm. But these objections wouldn't stop LaFrance — he knows the rig works.

Panfish Tips

Bobby Humphrey
Split-Shot Jigs

Fishing with jigs in brush and timber is the number-one way to take crappies in many reservoirs and rivers. The drawback of the method is that usually it means lots of lost lures; if you're fishing with commercially made jigs, the snags can get costly. Some anglers mold their own jigs with hot lead, but Bobby Humphrey, a taxidermist from Strawberry Plains, Tennessee, has a solution that's even cheaper and easier. Humphrey modifies a stout-wire hook, then attaches a single split-shot for a head. Jigs made this way cost only a few cents; besides, they snag less to begin with, since the hook is shorter than on a typical jig. Another bonus: the stout wire won't straighten out if you hook a big fish like a bass, as the thinner and softer wire of ordinary jig hooks will. Humphrey finishes the jig with his own special tail with plenty of action to attract crappies.

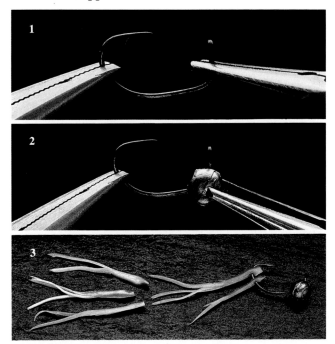

MAKE a split-shot jig by (1) bending the shank of an Eagle Claw 84 hook, size 4 or 6, to form a right angle about ⅛ inch from the eye. Before it's bent, the hook must be heated until red; but heating it too long will make it brittle. (2) Pinch a split-shot onto the bend just formed. The shot may then be painted, if desired. (3) Slice a 1½-inch squid tail into long strips, full length, then attach two or three strips onto the jig hook.

Charlie Ingram
Big Jigging Spoon for Crappies

Jigging spoons have more action than ordinary jigs, since their shape makes them flutter on the drop. In large sizes, they're popular vertical-jigging lures for bass schooling in deep timber during fall and winter. Charlie Ingram of Eufaula, Alabama, a guide on Lake Eufaula, has found that these same large spoons will take big crappies holding deep in heavy brush and treetops. His favorite is a ¾-ounce Hopkins with no dressing or bait on the treble. He

files the hook points to dull them slightly. The dull hooks are less likely to bite into woody cover and hang up, but are sharp enough to pierce the soft mouth of a crappie.

Mike McKee
Belly Strip for Big Perch

For yellow perch, the ideal natural bait is one that not only gets plenty of bites but also holds up well for fish after fish. After catching a perch, you need to get your bait back down to the school as quickly as possible, to keep them stirred up and feeding. Every time you stop to rebait, the fish start to lose interest. Mike McKee, a newspaper outdoor columnist from Michigan City, Indiana, fishes with a belly strip cut from a perch — a tough, appealing bait that will catch several fish before it's worn out. He rigs it on a size 6 or 8 hook. Two baits are fished at once, on a pair of droppers above a bell sinker. McKee works them just above the bottom, continually raising and lowering his rod tip a foot or two.

CUT a strip an inch long and ⅛ inch wide from the underside of a perch, just behind the anal fin. Leave a couple of rays from the tail fin attached to the strip. Hook the strip through its front end.

Trout & Salmon

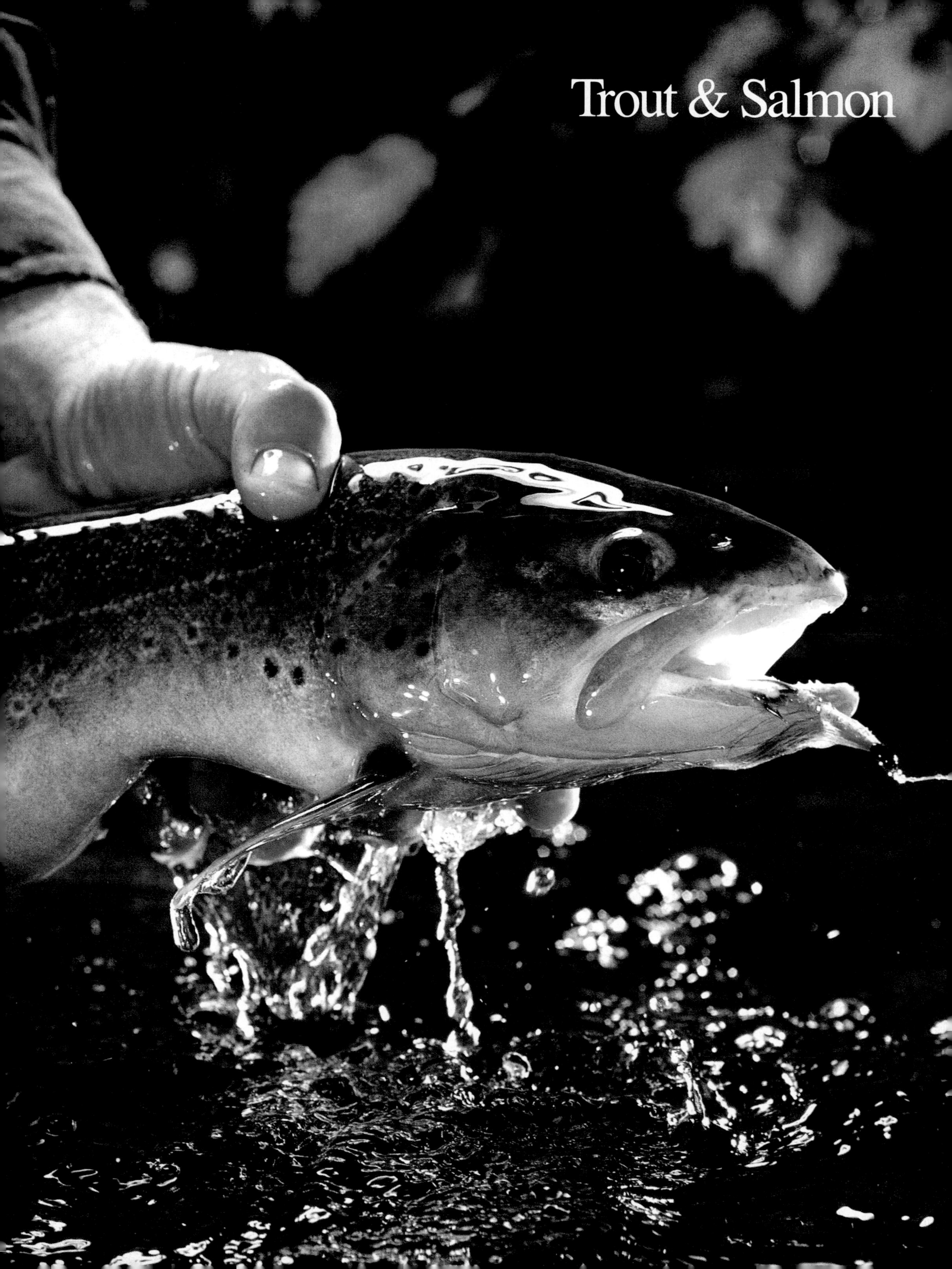

Movin' On for Tailwater Trophies

by Dick Sternberg

On a typical day, Carl Jones drifts 20 miles to catch world-class trout in tailwater streams

It didn't take Carl Jones long to convince me he was a pro. On the first cast of our three-day trip on Arkansas' famed White River, I hooked and landed a gorgeous 5-pound brown trout.

We had just motored away from the dock at White Hole Acres, Carl's base of operations. "Water's comin' already," Carl noted in his typical Ozark drawl. "We'll hafta fish fast and fish hard." I tied on a number 9 CountDown Rapala and cast toward the bank across from the dock. I made about six cranks, then *wham!*

And I'd always thought that fishing for big browns was tough.

Of course, the White River is famous for its trophy trout, so a fish like my 5-pounder doesn't raise an eyebrow. Since 1952, when the Bull Shoals Dam was completed, the White has produced a North American record brown trout no fewer than five times, the largest a 33-pound 8-ouncer in 1977.

Before the dam was built, the river held only warmwater fish. Cold water drawn from the depths of the reservoir now feeds the river and enables it to support trout.

"Guess I know the river well as anyone," Carl surmises. "Been fishin' it since I was a kid. My dad used to guide here starting back in the fifties, just after they built the dam. We guided together for eleven years, and he was real good competition. We'd find a bunch of good fish, then he'd fish for 'em one day and I'd fish for 'em the next. He taught me more about fishing than anybody."

One thing that separates Carl from most other guides on the river is his versatility. His strategy depends mainly on how much water is being discharged from the dam. When the lake is too high, or more power generation is needed, more water is discharged. "You got to fish different at different water stages," Carl explains. "The water level can

---

Carl Jones

Home: *Yellville, Arkansas*

Occupation: *Trout guide at White Hole Acres Resort near Flippin, Arkansas. Also guides deer and turkey hunters in the fall.*

In 23 years of guiding on the White River, Carl Jones has tallied 25 brown trout weighing over 20 pounds for his customers and himself. The heaviest fish of all, caught in 1976, weighed 30 pounds 2 ounces. And on September 19, 1987, he boated a 20-pound 12-ounce brown, a pending world record for 2-pound-test line.

"I'd been trying to break the 2-pound line record for seven years," Carl says. "Then one day when the water was low, I floated over a deep hole and spotted fifteen big browns. Threw out a blown-up crawler and it no more than hit the water when the big one grabbed it. I fought that fish for an hour and 45 minutes."

Carl can entertain you with fish tales all day as you float down the White. He'll tell you about 15-pound rainbows, 25-pound browns, and 10-pound cutthroats that live in different holes along the river. And he should know . . . he's caught and released a good share of them. "I ask my customers to throw back any big fish they don't want to mount. Most of them cooperate real good. They understand that fishing won't hold up if you keep those big ones. There's plenty of small rainbows for people who want a meal."

Early-morning low water on the White River, before release starts from dam

change as much as 18 feet overnight. Where you caught fish one day can be dry land the next.

"Love to fish low water," he says. "Seventeen of my 25 biggest browns were caught when the river was down. Water's usually lowest in summer, but it can be low anytime the weather's been dry.

"Best time for big trout is June and July," he continues. "When the gates are shut, the downstream water warms up and the trout are forced to move toward the dam where the water is cooler. They're concentrated in a smaller area, so they're a lot easier to get at.

"When you're fishing low water, trout seem to bite best right in the middle of the day. You'd think it'd be just the opposite. But when the water's higher, time of day doesn't seem to make much difference.

"Nice thing about low water is you can see where they're at. They get schooled up in certain holes, and if you know where they are, you can catch a bunch. I like a calm, clear day because you can see 'em a lot better. If it's windy, you can't spot 'em."

When Carl is scouting for trout, he stands on the rear seat of his boat and steers the outboard with his foot. "Yeah, I've gone in a few times, but it's the best way to see the trout," he maintains. "You've got to look way ahead of the boat — they won't sit still and let you drift over them. They're real spooky because the water's so clear.

"Once you find some, the best way is to anchor above a hole and throw bait at 'em. If there's a lot of trout in the hole, I'll wait 'em out. Sometime during the day, one of 'em's gonna feed. If there's only a fish or two, then I'll move to another hole where I've seen some.

"I use the same rig for most any kind of bait. It's just a dropper rig with a number 7 to 10 bell sinker — depending on depth and current speed — and a hook. "If I'm after big fish, I'll put two big crawlers on the hook. Another good big-fish bait is sewed-on sculpins. You can pick 'em up on certain flats after the water has been high for a few days and then drops fast. You've got to fish 'em dead. First thing a live one'll do is swim under a rock and hang you up. Softshell craws work good, too."

For live-bait fishing, Carl prefers a light spinning outfit. He normally uses 6-pound monofilament, but goes as light as 2-pound when the fish are extra-spooky. "Don't use anything lighter than 6-pound for sculpin fishing," he advises. "A big brown'll mouth a sculpin and then chew on it; and when he turns, his teeth'll fray the line."

Using two anchors, Carl positions his boat broadside to the current just upstream from a hole where he has seen trout. Anchoring broadside makes it easier for two or three people to fish the hole, but is not recommended in fast current. As a safety precaution, Carl ties both anchor lines to the boat with slip knots. This way, he can untie them quickly should the current pick up and threaten to overturn the boat.

Navigating the White River in low water can be treacherous. Carl, and practically everyone else who fishes the river regularly, uses a special boat originally designed by Carl's father. It looks like a long, skinny jonboat, with a length of 20 feet but a beam of only 4 feet. Both ends are swept up so the bow won't take on water; the stern can be maneuvered easily with a paddle. The fiberglass hull draws only a few inches of water, for skimming over gravel bars, and its thin shape makes it easy to steer

How to Make a Dropper Rig for Live Bait

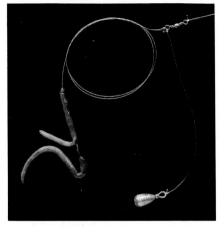

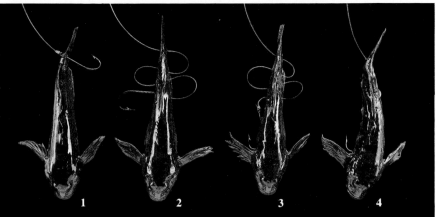

TIE rig as shown with 6-pound mono and size 4 long-shank hook. Thread one crawler up line; another over hook.

HOOK a sculpin on same type of rig by (1) inserting a size 4 long-shank hook through base of tail, then (2) back through body three times. (3) Push hook through side so point protrudes behind pectoral fin. (4) Snug up line.

How Jones Fishes at Low Water

USE a narrow, shallow-draft jonboat for navigating in low water. A boat of this design will steer easily through narrow chutes, and will float over shallow bars.

LOOK for trout while motoring downstream. Jones wears polarized sunglasses and stands on the boat seat so he can see into the water. Avoid motoring over the fish.

ANCHOR just upstream of a pool where trout were spotted. Jones uses two anchors to keep the boat broadside to the current so two anglers can fish the hole effectively.

PULL hooked fish away from the hole quickly so you don't spook the others. The bell-sinker rig with two crawlers or a sculpin works best for trout during low water.

Sternberg's first-cast brown

through narrow chutes. The boat is powered by a 15-horsepower outboard.

Rising water is another story, a race against time. When Carl tells you "water's comin' already," he means the dam gates are open and the water is rising fast. When he says "we'll hafta fish fast and fish hard," he means the river will soon be too high to fish effectively, so you'll have to motor downstream quickly to stay ahead of the swelling water, stopping to fish some likely spots along the way.

Carl calls this technique "fishing the bulge," the bulge being the advancing surge of high water. "The bulge seems to turn the fish on," he explains. "If you can get on at just the right time and ride it, you'll catch more trout than you would at low water."

When you stop to fish a spot, the bulge catches up with you in a hurry. You can tell when it arrives by watching the clarity. When the White is low it's very clear, but when it starts rising it gets murkier and you'll see bits of weeds and algae floating downstream. "When you start to see a lot of trash, you've got to run down and get away from it," Carl says. "Otherwise the trout can't see your bait too good, and it'll pick up lots of weeds.

"When I'm fishing the bulge, I like to throw a CountDown Rapala, either size 7 or 9. Rapalas are big-fish baits, and a lot of guys don't have the patience to throw them all day. But if you're after big trout, they work a lot better than live bait. Early in the season, silver works best because the trout are eating shad. By June, they start eating creek minnows which are gold-colored, so I switch to a gold CountDown. The big browns can be real particular — color makes a big difference."

For casting Rapalas, Carl uses a 5½-foot medium-action baitcasting outfit spooled with 8-pound-test

How Jones Fishes the Bulge

BEGIN fishing just downstream of the bulge. The location of the bulge may not be immediately apparent, but if the bulge passes you, the water will carry bits of weed that catch on the hooks of your lure.

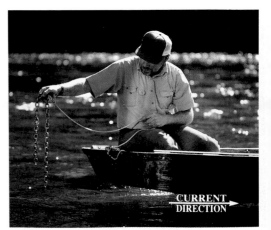

LOWER a drag chain off the bow as you start drifting. The chain will keep the bow pointed upstream.

mono. In this type of fishing, he says any line lighter than 8-pound will snap too easily when you set the hook.

"Cast just downstream of the boat, let the plug sink a few seconds, then twitch it hard a few times before you start to reel," Carl suggests. "Browns usually hit just when you start reeling. But don't twitch when you're fishing rainbows.

"I throw out a drag chain to slow my drift. This gives you more time to work your spot, plus it keeps the bow pointing upstream so the boat stays at the same angle. When I'm running over deep water, I just leave the chain out. The rope's short enough so the chain doesn't get in the motor. In shallow water, I pull it in just to be safe. The chain works real good. In fact, a lot of fly fishermen want to see it banned. They say a chain rips up too many weeds on the bottom, but they rip up just as many when they're wading.

"When I'm fishing the bulge, I always look for break-offs. You know — spots where a rock pile or a bar drops into deeper water. The drop may be only 8 inches, but that's enough to hold trout. They rest in the deeper water because there's less current. Usually, they're not far from the deep pools where you find 'em when the water's low."

High water — after the bulge has rolled on past — presents yet another set of challenges. "Most important thing to remember when the water's high is to cast close to the bank," Carl advises. "Not as much current in there, so it's the best place for trout to rest. The higher the water, the closer you need to cast.

"I use pretty much the same technique I do for fishing the bulge, but instead of throwing a Count-Down I may throw a Shad Rap. The big bill makes

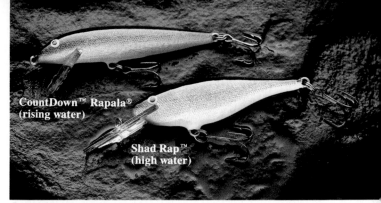

Jones' favorite plugs

it run deeper, and it starts diving as soon as you reel it away from the bank, so the big trout can see it. If the water's not too high I'll go with a number 7 Shad Rap, but when it's really high, I switch to a number 8.

"When all the gates are open, the current rolls along at 5 or 6 miles an hour. Before you know it, you're 20 miles downstream, and it'll take you the rest of the day to motor back up. If you plan on floating with the current, get a buddy to meet you at a downstream landing with a trailer. That way you can fish a lot longer.

"If the water's already high when I start fishing, I usually float a ways, then run back up and float again. Never try to anchor in high water. Current's fast enough to suck your bow under. Hardly a year goes by when I don't pull somebody out of the river after they anchored their boat and it turned over in the current.

"Personally, I'd much rather fish when the water's low. The fast current makes it tough to get your lure deep enough, 'specially when the trout are tucked up tight to the bank."

It's probably a good thing the water gets high once in a while. The White River trout can enjoy life a lot more when Carl's working on his garden.

ANGLE your cast just downstream of the boat, using a CountDown Rapala. When casting downstream, the plug has a chance to sink before the line tightens up.

TWITCH the rod hard several times as the plug is sinking. The twitching action seems to attract big browns, which often strike when you start to retrieve.

(1) Deep-water chart recorder; (2) radar, for low-visibility navigation; (3) Loran-C, for navigating, staying on fish schools, and reading over-the-bottom trolling speed; (4) radio direction finder for locating other boats; (5) depth, temperature, and speed indicator; (6) video recorder, for shallower water; (7) marine radio.

Science Vs. Salmon

by Jake Barnes

Captain John Oravec unleashes his arsenal of modern equipment and technical know-how on Great Lakes salmon

It is mid-August, the heart of the summer king season, and at 4:30 in the morning John Oravec and his mate, Jessie the wonder dog, board the *Troutman*. Jessie takes his elevated seat on the port side and falls asleep. John gets to work.

He strips old line from two reels, and spools on new. As he finishes mopping the aft deck, voices cut through the fog. The clients have arrived. The day begins.

While the five fishermen drink coffee and swap lies, John eases the *Troutman* out of the harbor and heads offshore — ten miles offshore, where the king salmon loll away their summer feeding on alewives, the last feast before the ardors of the fall spawning run.

Not many years ago, summer on Lake Ontario was a time for salmon fishermen to patch up gear and dream of fall. Between spring, when kings worked the shallows, and fall, when they returned to the rivers, they simply disappeared. So John and another captain set out to find them.

They started cruising, eyes locked on graphs, fingers poised by Loran-C navigators to mark the position of whatever they found. Ultimately they wandered far offshore, where smaller boats couldn't go. "There's a lot of water out there, and a lot of it was empty," remembers Oravec of those futile days of searching the 7500-square-mile lake.

But finally the searching paid off. "We found fish ten miles out. Salmon like a relatively shallow

John Oravec

Home: *Kendall, New York*

Occupation: *Fishing guide on Lake Ontario, the Finger Lakes, and the St. Lawrence River; owner of Tight Lines Charter Service, Kent, New York*

John Oravec grew up in Port Clinton, Ohio and in Rochester, New York, before the Great Lakes fisheries were rejuvenated. Oravec attended Wash-ington State University, where he developed a taste for salmon fishing; he graduated in biology from a small college in Rochester. Unable to find a job as a fisheries biologist, he went to work in the animal unit of the Cardiac Research Center at the University of Rochester.

In his spare time he began to guide for lake trout on the Finger Lakes and for muskies on the St. Lawrence. As the salmon fishery developed in Lake Ontario,

Oravec was there to pioneer it. In 1977 he made the leap to full-time guiding. He pursues salmon from April to September, then turns to muskies.

Oravec started guiding for salmon with a 17-foot outboard boat. Today, that 17-footer has been replaced by the Troutman, a 10-meter Trojan International with twin 350-horsepower engines. The boat is equipped with practically every conceivable type of electronic gadgetry.

Most Great Lakes charter captains have a reputation for being tight-lipped with fishing information, but not Oravec. "I don't mind sharing information," he says. "There's a lot of water and a lot of fish out there. I may be putting myself out of business and other people in business, but I like to see other folks enjoy good fishing. Stocking salmon costs a lot of money, and if more people enjoy the fishing, the politicians will provide more funding for the programs."

thermocline, 40 to 80 feet down, and we began to find that the thermocline became shallower as we moved farther offshore. Over 500 to 600 feet of water, we discovered what I call 'temperature ridges,' which are big mounds of cold water surrounded by warmer water. The ridges are easy to find with a graph recorder because they're covered with schools of alewives. Some of these ridges are only large enough for a couple of boats to work, others are several miles long.

"So out there, where no one had fished seriously before, were the two things that salmon needed: cold water and lots of food. And there were the salmon, not massed together like they are in the fall but cruising alone, big gypsy fish picking off bait when the mood struck.

"Not that they're always easy to locate. We soon found that wind moves the cold-water masses and the salmon move with them. The challenge at the start of each day is to figure out which way they've moved. The best way is to cruise around with a graph and find the schools of alewives — the salmon won't be far away. The captains work together to find the fish, then we share the information. There's too much water to cover by yourself."

Eight miles out now, and the depth approaches 500 feet. John has the video and the chart recorder on, marking clouds of bait and a few large fish. He spots another charter a mile ahead. He gets on the radio and chats with the captain, who fished these same waters the day before. The captain, a good pal, tells him the salmon are on a bite at 46 feet. John thanks him, asks one of the clients to take the wheel, and heads to the stern to rig up.

Oravec sets stern downriggers

The *Troutman* carries seven Cannon Digi-Troll downriggers: one each on the port and starboard side, equipped with extension arms, and five more across the stern. All have digital control pads. The boat also has two 24-foot outriggers — aluminum poles equipped with pulley devices to carry lines away from the boat's wake. The poles stand vertically when not in use and swing out to the side when fishing. The outriggers will not be used today, but John will rig both of the side-mounted downriggers, and four downriggers on the stern.

In addition, he will rig two lines with Dipsy Divers, weighted plastic devices that attach to the line and pull it down and to the side of the boat. The dive angle can be adjusted to control how far to the side the device will track. Normally a Dipsy must be used with a fairly short leader, but Oravec rigs it so the leader can be set to any length (photo at right). Two other lines will be rigged with drop weights, 6- to 22-ounce lead balls rigged with a release that allows them to drop off the line when a fish strikes.

The lines rigged with the Dipsy Divers and drop weights are intended to pick up kings that Oravec wouldn't get with the downriggers. "The Dipsies widen your trolling path and pick up high-riding kings," he explains. "They work best at depths of 35 feet or less. Kings in shallow water spook from the boat, but with the lines out to the side, spooking doesn't seem to be a problem.

"The drop weights are very effective for big kings, which tend to get real choosy at times. They might not come up for the cannonballs. If I'm fishing, say, 50 feet down, the drop weight would be about 150 feet behind the boat. You get to know how deep they go by experience. With drop weights, you're fishing for the fish twice — if they ignore the first set of lures that come by, you've got a chance with the second set.

"If the fish are hitting on the drop weights, I may rig an extra set of drop weights on the outriggers.

"With Dipsies and drop weights, I use Daiwa 47LC counter reels so if the fish start hitting, I can drop back to exactly the same depth."

Line-counter reel

Because Oravec can run so many lines and because he's aware of all the variables — depth, "lead" (distance from cannonball to lure), lure selection, trolling speed, trolling pattern — he's had to adopt a very systematic approach. It's a methodology that hearkens to his days as a scientist, where controlling the variables and carefully noting results were the crux of effective research.

How Oravec Rigs His Dipsy Divers

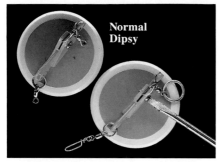

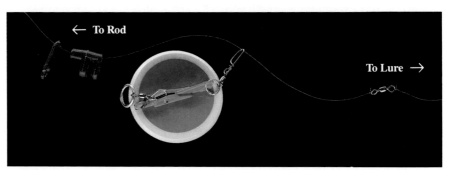

ADD large ring to front swivel; replace rear swivel with snap-swivel. Cut rings open; solder shut. Tighten screw so release will not trip.

THREAD the pin and body of a Jettison Release onto the line; clip on the Dipsy Diver, using the snap-swivel. Tie the line to a barrel swivel large enough that it will not slip through the snap-swivel on the Dipsy. Tie the leader to the barrel swivel.

POSITION the Dipsy as far up the line as desired. Place the large split-ring on the Dipsy in the slot in the body of the Jettison Release; insert the peg into the hole. The Dipsy is now secured on the line.

A STRIKE will pop the pin out of the body of the Jettison Release. The Dipsy will then slide down the line, stopping at the barrel swivel. If the Dipsy wouldn't slide on the line, you could not use as long a leader because the Dipsy would prevent you from reeling in close enough to net the fish.

How Oravec Rigs His Drop Weights

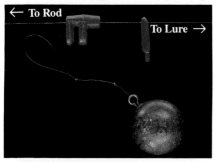

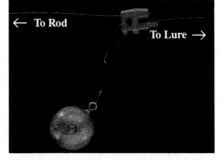

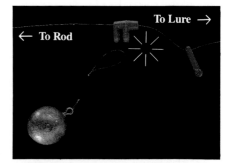

THREAD a Jettison Release onto the line. Tie 17-pound mono to a lead ball, then make a loop in the end.

SET the release in the desired position, place the loop in the slot, then insert the peg in the hole.

A STRIKE pops the peg, and the ball falls to the bottom. You can fight the fish without the heavy sinker.

But before he brings all the high-tech gear into play and cranks up his awesome fish-catching computer of a brain, John takes care of the little stuff — the grist of so many magazine articles and the bane of so many fishermen. Every day, before a lure hits the water, he inspects the guides on each rod for rough spots that might cut line. He checks the leader and line on each reel.

All tackle is clean, lubricated, and sturdy. John's rods for downriggers and drop weights are 8-foot Shakespeare Ugly Stiks, models 1131 and 1101, with medium-light action. He matches these rods with Shimano level-wind reels — 300 Tritons and TLD 2000 Charter specials. For Dipsy Divers, he makes his own rods, 10-footers with a stiffer action. He uses green 17-pound Trilene XT on the downrigger and drop-weight rods; green 25-pound Trilene XT on the Dipsy rods.

Nothing is taken for granted. Everything is meticulously maintained. If you or I lose a fish to a faulty piece of gear, we have no one to blame but ourselves; if one of John's clients loses a fish the same way, he'll curse the captain forever. John can't afford curses. Fishing already is tough enough.

John makes sure that a selection of spoons hangs on a rack by the wheel, all within easy reach; others swing from a rack in the stern. On most of the spoons he's replaced the stock hooks with the best stainless hooks he can buy. For better hooking, he often removes the factory treble hooks and substitutes a single hook, but only if the single still balances the spoon for proper action. Hooks are sharpened with a file and tested by scratching a thumbnail each time a spoon goes into the water. Terminal tackle is kept to a minimum. The leader is tied directly to the split-ring on the spoon, and then to a ball-bearing swivel 3 to 4 feet back. If the swivel were clipped directly to the spoon, it might inhibit the spoon's action.

The type of spoon Oravec uses in summer depends on the size of the baitfish the kings are eating. "If they're feeding on immature alewives, 1 to 2½ inches, I use small spoons like the Pirate 44, and 2F or 3F Evil Eye. If they're eating bigger alewives, I use a Northern King 28, Pirate 55, or Evil Eye 5F.

"Starting about August 1, you start seeing mature salmon. They're bigger than the run-of-the mill fish, their color is darker, and they're starting to go off feed. You have to give these fish something with a more erratic, exaggerated action, like a dodger with a squid, fly, or spoon."

Oravec's Terminal Tackle for King Salmon

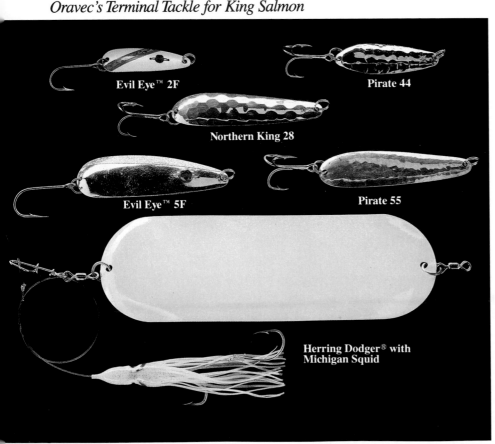

APPLY prism tape to spoons to vary brightness and color. Trim along spoon edge using razor blade.

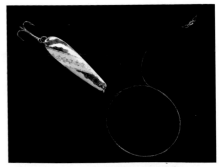

TIE one end of leader to ring on spoon; other end to swivel. A snap-swivel on spoon would spoil action.

Oravec's favorite salmon lures

How Oravec Rigs His Trolling Spread

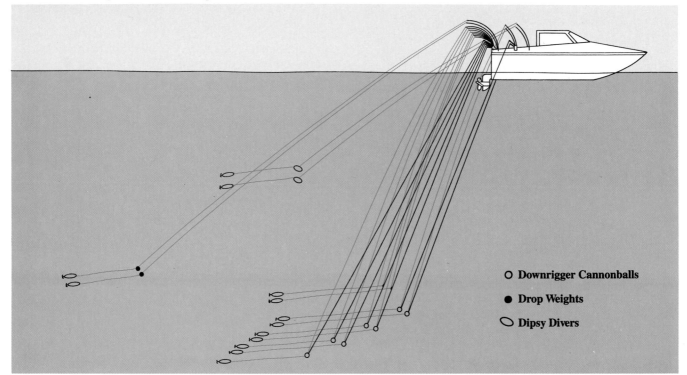

○ **Downrigger Cannonballs**

● **Drop Weights**

⬭ **Dipsy Divers**

SIDE VIEW. The downrigger lines, including the "stackers" (p. 122), run farthest forward, the drop-weight lines farthest back. The Dipsy lines run in between. At times, salmon may refuse to hit the downrigger lines running beneath the boat, but they may strike Dipsy lines farther to the side, or drop-weight lines farther to the rear.

REAR VIEW. Downriggers are set in a V pattern, with the center bomb deepest, the outside bombs shallowest. Stackers on corner downriggers are 10 to 15 feet higher than bombs. Dipsies run shallower than other lines. Drop weights run almost as deep as downrigger bombs.

TOP VIEW (with outriggers rigged). With outrigger lines, the boat covers a 50- to 60-foot swath. The outrigger lines are rigged with drop weights. The Dipsies run to the side, but not as far as the outriggers. The downrigger lines are evenly spaced across boat's width.

As for color selection, Oravec recommends bright colors like silver in early morning or in murky water, and darker colors in bright sunlight or in clear water. "You need some flash in the dark environment so salmon can see it," he maintains. "Then as the sun comes up, I use darker lures or a silver lure with a dark stripe on it to tone it down."

To most fishermen, what goes on the end of the line seems the key to success; it's the variable most often changed, twiddled, and discussed. But Oravec has a different view. On most days he sticks with lures that have proven themselves over time. Often, he rigs all six downriggers with the same spoon. He may vary the size a bit and he might run one spoon with green prism tape, and another with black. This approach helps him concentrate on finding the right presentation, rather than the "secret" lure.

Downriggers are set in a *V* with the middle stern downriggers running deepest, the outer stern 'riggers and side-mounted 'riggers shallowest. This enables John to turn the boat without tangling the lines. All lines have a lead of 20 to 40 feet.

Sometimes Oravec runs "stackers" to improve his odds. A stacker is a second line attached to a movable release on the downrigger cable, usually 10 to 15 feet above the main line. He normally stacks only the corner downriggers to minimize tangling problems.

John likes to involve his clients in the rigging, so they feel they're really fishing. He tells them to measure out line by grasping the line at the reel and stripping forward until their hand hits the first guide. That's 2 feet. Ten strips, and the line is out 20 feet. All the downrigger lines are set in Roemer releases. Oravec prefers Roemers because they do not scuff or twist the line like most other releases.

Miraculously, the downriggers are set within minutes. The inside spoons run at 50 feet, the outside spoons at 42 feet. The ones in the middle split the distance. Before lowering the corner downriggers, Oravec attaches stackers 10 feet above the lines attached at the cannonballs.

Next John sets out the two rods rigged with Dipsies. He lets out 110 feet of line on each rod, which he figures will take the Dipsy down 30 feet, based on the angle at which it is set to dive.

The clients settle back in their chairs, cradling their coffee mugs and buying the affections of Jessie the wonder dog with bits of stale doughnut. John returns to the helm and gets to work. It's from this position behind the wheel that he fishes. He may not reel in the fish; but he finds them, he

presents the lures to them, and, since he's constantly watching the rigs and is usually the first person to see a strike, he often sets the hook.

John trolls on one engine. To keep the boat speed slow enough, he uses trolling plates. The plates

Trolling plates (arrows) in raised position

attach to the transom and are lowered with a handle to create more water resistance. "Trolling speed is the number-one variable in fishing for kings. You have to experiment each day to find the right speed for the conditions. Most of the time, I want a lure speed of 1.9 to 2.4 knots. But it's not how fast you're moving over the surface that counts, it's the speed over the bottom. Lots of times you're bucking wind-generated surface currents, so your speed over the bottom is different than what it appears to be on the surface." Oravec has a digital surface-speed indicator, but to determine true trolling speed over the bottom, he relies on his Loran-C navigator. And he knows — to the tenth — the ranges in which his various lures run best.

He settles in at 2.2 knots, checks the set astern, quickly goes aft to increase the line tension on one rod, returns to the helm, spots a cloud of bait on the graph, and marks the location on the Loran. He cuts the wheel slightly to turn the spoons as they cut by the bait: this simulates individual baitfish breaking away from the rest, and seems to trigger strikes. Then he checks the set again, and spots a trembling rod tip.

"We're going through bait," he announces to the fishermen. "Watch it — ." And with that, a rod releases and Oravec sounds, "Fish on!"

It's a good king. John reaches the rod before any of the clients, pulls it out of the holder, takes up the slack, and sets the hook. A client steps over and John hands him the rod. The client watches in amazement as the fish smokes 150 yards of line from the reel. Finally, the run stops and John begins coaching.

"Pump him, pump him. Reel only after the pump. If the fish is taking out line, don't crank on him. There, that's it. Now you've got it."

In ten minutes the king is on the surface. Oravec sees that the fish will come to the starboard side, so he barks short, efficient orders to the other fishermen. "Release the line on the outboard downrigger. Bring up the ball. Okay, let's pull up that outside rig on the stern." Nothing is left to chance. The man fighting the fish has plenty of room to maneuver, yet half the lines still are in the water, fishing.

As the king comes in, John reaches for the starboard net. He carries a net on each side, a big net with a 3-foot-deep bag. He tells the client to step to the stern and take in line. The fish is worn out and planing. John directs the client to raise his rod tip and take a half step back, which brings the fish deftly into the waiting net. A 26-pound king.

As the clients admire the catch, John tends to business, muttering to himself. "Hit that one at 46 feet. Lead was 30 feet. A silver Pirate spoon with green tape." All this goes into the computer.

John directs the clients to kill the fish before trying to remove the hook. He has seen a big salmon lunge and drive a treble hook into a hand. As soon as the spoon is free, John checks the line and leader for nicks, and sharpens the hooks. Then he adjusts all the lines on the starboard side to match the one that was hit. He lengthens the leads, puts on identical spoons and tightens up the downrigger spread around that 46-foot depth. He doesn't touch the port side. That's his control. Those rigs will remain the same until he sees more of a pattern emerge.

The bite is on, and two more kings come to the boat before life slows down. In the next hour, yet another king is taken. Then everything stops. This is when most of us stick with what we've been doing and blame our bad luck on the fickle nature of fish, or call it a day and head home. But not John. First, he runs through the circumstances of each catch, which he remembers in detail: the exact location (Loran helps here), the depth of each lure, the trolling speed, the lead. Inside, outside, port or stern downrigger, Dipsy or drop weight. Then he gets on the horn and checks with other captains. At what depth have they been catching fish? At what speed?

Soon patterns emerge. The fish appear to be deeper, so the downriggers are let down farther. The sun is high overhead, so darker spoons are in order. The Dipsy and drop-weight rigs are being hit more often than the downriggers: John believes the salmon are boat-shy today, so he rigs another line with a drop weight that he can run 100 feet behind the boat.

He spots a slick of weeds and debris on the water. He knows from past experience that kings hang around these slicks. He raises two lines to 20 feet and works the slick's edge: "Fish on!"

John Oravec makes things happen. If his best attempts are stymied, he doesn't get discouraged. He looks for an explanation. Like the scientist he is, he learns what he can from defeat. He constantly asks himself probing questions: Where are the fish? If they're not here, where would they be? If they're feeding, what are they feeding on and how can I best approximate that food? And if they're feeding, why aren't they taking my lures? What was special about the lure they did hit? If they aren't feeding, how can I provoke them into a strike?

Question, analyze, question, analyze: for John Oravec it never stops. Notwithstanding the array of high-tech wizardry he's installed, the most important piece of equipment on the *Troutman*, and the most impressive, is the humming computer between his ears.

For big kings, Oravec prefers a long-handled net with a deep bag

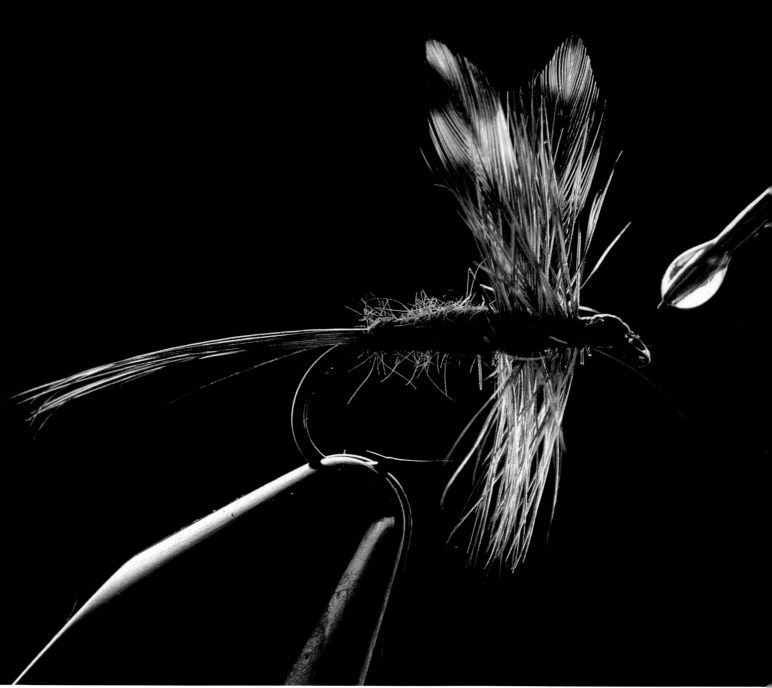

Putting the finishing touches on an Adams

Ed Van Put

Home: *Livingston Manor, New York*

Occupation: *Principal Fish and Wildlife Technician for the New York State Department of Environmental Conservation*

Ed Van Put was born and raised in northern New Jersey. "I started out with flies for bass and sunfish when I was thirteen," he recalls. "I wasn't much interested in trout fishing at the time, because in New Jersey it was all put-and-take. They put fish in on Thursday,

and you caught them on Friday. So I never could understand all the hoopla about trout fishing.

"After I got out of the Army, I read some articles about trout fishing in the Catskills and decided to try it. Before long, I was coming up here every weekend. I moved here in 1962."

Today, Ed Van Put is a superb fly fisherman and fly tier who's celebrated for fishing mainly with a single fly pattern, the Adams. Lee Wulff, the famed fly-fishing innovator who lives close by in the Catskills, described Ed as "probably the finest of all the Catskill fly fishermen." Wulff once wrote that when he watches Ed fish, "I am

The Universal Fly?

by Robert H. Boyle

*Ed Van Put, Catskill fly-fisherman supreme, relies heavily
on a single fly pattern — the Adams*

It was a September afternoon at Shaver's Pool on the upper Beaverkill; the sun was bright and the water low and clear. But these difficult conditions didn't bother Ed Van Put.

Ed's first half-dozen casts into the pool with a size 16 Adams brought no response, but instead of changing to a different fly, he went down in size to an 18 Adams as a few small caddisflies started coming off. The hatch remained sparse for the next couple of hours, but despite taking time out to explain his techniques in detail and all the while using only an Adams, he landed and released three dozen wild and stocked trout. They were brooks, browns, and rainbows, the largest 12 inches. He appeared to catch fish at will. "I'm surprised when a feeding fish doesn't take my fly," he remarked at one point. But the catch fell short of his personal best for the pool — 54 fish in two hours, all on the Adams.

The Beaverkill is perhaps the East's most famous trout stream. It also may be the most heavily fished. To catch 54 "educated" trout in two hours is a remarkable feat. Ed Van Put performs such feats with consistency. And he performs them with what most fly-fishing experts would regard as simplistic methods — simplistic but extremely effective.

"I don't market the Adams, I don't get a commission," he said, "but it's the fly that works most often. When I'm fishing dry, I use an Adams about 90 percent of the time. The Adams looks like a lot of naturals. It has that blue-gray-brown color. It definitely has something going for it. I don't think that you could take just any other fly and say, 'This is all I'm going to use to catch fish,' and be a success with it." Most of the time, Van Put fishes the Adams on a 6-weight double-taper floating line with a 5X leader.

reminded of a cat stalking a bird; in him I see the same intentness and singleness of purpose."

When the Catskill Fly Fishing Center invited former President Jimmy Carter to give the address at a $500-a-plate fund-raising dinner, Ed was chosen to serve as his guide.

In his state job, Ed specializes in purchasing public fishing easements from landowners along streams. The work gives him almost as much pleasure as fishing. "When you procure a mile, say, of the Callicoon Creek and know that people will be able to fish it, you get great satis-

faction knowing you created public use for all time."

During his off hours, Ed does stream-improvement work for a number of Catskill fishing clubs and private landowners, including Laurance S. Rockefeller, who owns Shaver's Pool and six miles of the upper Beaverkill. He has also taught classes at Lee and Joan Wulff's fly-fishing school.

Ed uses a Vince Cummings one-piece 8-foot glass rod. "It's all I fish with," he explained. "I have three of them. I fish almost every day, and if I used a two-piece rod I'd wear out the ferrules in a year or two. I just don't like graphite — it's too stiff. Graphite rods are great to cast because you can get more distance out of them, but they're very unforgiving. With graphite, I've seen more people bust off on the strike, leave flies in the fish, and what not. But glass, like bamboo, is soft. If you strike too hard it will flex rather than snap the tippet."

Van Put demonstrates the flex in his Vince Cummings rod

Ed began using the Adams consistently a couple of years after he moved to the Catskills. At first he tied imitations of specific naturals and, in his words, "ran around with boxes full of flies." He also kept a detailed fishing diary on water conditions, what he caught, and what he caught them on; the catch records showed that the Adams was by far the most effective dry fly. "From then on," Ed said, "I just kept the Adams on, and instead of stopping every ten minutes to change flies like most fishermen do, all I had to do was to remember how many fish I'd caught for the day.

"The most important thing on the Adams is the wings," Ed said. "In one day I caught 37 fish on one Adams. The tail came off, the body came off.

That was all right because the fly continued to catch fish. The last fish I caught on it was a 17½-inch brown. And by then, the damned fly — all it was, was a pair of wings."

To be successful, an Adams must have the right proportions and materials. By his own admission, Ed is "very fussy" about his flies. The feathers come from Plymouth Rock roosters he keeps in cages at his home in Livingston Manor. The wings are saddle-hackle tips he cuts from the birds in the fall, when the tips have the best shape and stiffness.

Getting the right materials and proportions for the Adams is only part of the battle. What remains is proper presentation. "The first step in presentation is position," Ed said. "To me, the ideal position to stand is across from the fish, maybe slightly downstream. What I try to do is show the fish only the fly, not

Hand-picking a hackle

the leader. I want the fly to come down right in front of him. I'm going to get the least amount of drag from this position, and I'm going to have the best angle to set the hook in the side of his jaw. The more upstream you cast, the more likely the leader will drift down to the trout ahead of the fly. The problem is not so much that the fish sees the leader — although he may — but that he bumps the leader on the rise, and this pulls the fly away.

How Van Put Ties an Adams

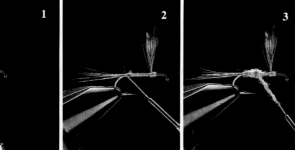

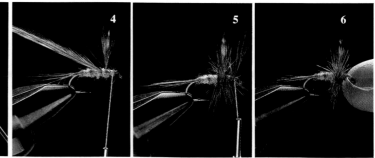

WRAP (1) thread onto hook, and tie on two grizzly hackle tips so they flare slightly. Wings should equal hook shank in length. (2) Wind thread to hook bend and tie in a dozen stiff brown and grizzly hackle fibers. Tail should be same length as shank. (3) Spin muskrat-fur dubbing onto thread, then wrap forward, making the body thicker at front. (4) Tie in two stiff grizzly hackles; wrap dubbing near eye. (5) Wind hackles on, making two turns behind the wings, two more between them, then two in front. Hackle fibers should extend just beyond wings. Wind thread over hackle stubs; trim them off. (6) Tie off thread with half-hitches. Apply cement to head.

"The problem with casting downstream is that you can take the fly out of the fish's mouth when you strike." With that, he cast downstream, a trout struck, and then the fly pulled out. Ed gave a loud laugh and exclaimed, "See, bad position!

"Another point that's very important to me — it may be obvious, but your first cast to a feeding fish should be your best cast. Most good fishermen do very little false casting. They make one false cast and then put the fly on the water, to get the fly and the fish on a collision course. In other words, if there were a fish out there" — he pointed to a spot 20 feet directly across stream — "and he were rising and rising, then the more you cast at that fish, the less likely you'd take him, because you're going to make a mistake. You're going to hit the water hard with your line, you're going to drag the fly in front of him, or whatever.

"Watch a feeding fish. He comes up, takes, and goes down; he comes up, takes, and goes down. You get his rhythm or timing figured out. You can usually tell whether he's a brown or a rainbow. A brown will keep rising in the same spot, a rainbow will move around a lot more.

"Now what you want to do is get in position, time that fish, and drop the fly right in front of him as close as you can without startling him, and without showing him any leader. You want that timing to be right so the fly and fish are on a collision course. Do that, and in my experience he's going to take the fly. He really is.

"A lot of people cast too far above a feeding fish. When they do, the fish may be going down by the time their fly gets to him. A fisherman thinks, 'Ah, he didn't want that fly,' and then starts thinking about changing flies. But the problem was, the fisherman didn't get the fly to the fish on a collison course.

"The timing of the cast," Ed noted, "depends on the hatch, how many flies are on the water. The more flies there are, then the more fish will feed, and the more heavily each one will feed. Take a fish like that one there ..." The trout was rising every ten seconds. Ed timed his cast, and his Adams touched down a few inches above the fish. "Ah, got him," he said. It was a 12-inch male brook trout in spawning colors. "As I was saying, you watch that rhythm, time the fish, and get that fly and the fish on a collision course as soon as possible."

When he's fishing dry, which he does about 60 percent of the time, Van Put occasionally will use some pattern other than the Adams. But he does so only for a definite, specific reason, as a result of closely observing the stream. He never switches from one fly to another at random, just chucking it and chancing

it, as most anglers do. "When midges are on the water, I'll use a 22 midge. I like a little midge called the Pheasant Tail, an old English fly. Dun hackle, and two fibers from a cock pheasant — one wound on for a body, one for a tail. That's all I ever use when I'm midging."

When fishing wet flies, he uses a Leadwing Coachman and a Royal Coachman, both at once. "I use the two patterns in tandem about 20 inches apart, the Leadwing on the tippet, the Royal on the dropper, a kind of traditional Catskill Irish way of doing things. With wet flies, I mostly fish down and across.

"Sometimes a Royal Coachman wet works even better than the Adams," Ed explained. "In early spring, when the water is high and discolored, it

How to Tie and Fish a Tandem Wet Fly Rig

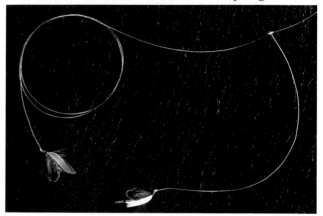

BLOOD-KNOT a 20-inch tippet to your leader, leaving one tag end untrimmed for a dropper. Tie a Leadwing Coachman on the tippet, a Royal Coachman on the dropper.

STRIP line in short pulls as the flies swing downstream into pockets where fish lie. The pulls make the flies twitch like natural nymphs swimming toward the surface.

FLIES that Van Put uses to supplement the (1) Adams include: (2) Pheasant Tail, (3) Leadwing Coachman, (4) Royal Coachman, (5) Zug Bug, (6) Black Ghost, (7) Muddler Minnow, and (8) Vamp.

gives you extra visibility. It also works well when the water temperature is 50 to 65 degrees, and there's no surface activity. I've caught a lot of fish on it. Sure, it's pretty — but it works, too.

"When there's no hatch or when a hatch is just beginning, I like to twitch the flies to the fish. The twitches draw more strikes because they make the flies resemble nymphs rising from the bottom to emerge. Once the hatch is in full swing, I'll switch back to the Adams."

His favorite nymph is a weighted Zug Bug, a pattern tied mainly of peacock herl. "With nymphs, I fish upstream with a short line, say 15 feet, keeping as much line off the water as possible. A short line gives you better control. You can't see the fish take the nymph, so you're concentrating on either a strike indicator or the tip of your line. You take in line at a constant rate of speed, so if it stops or hesitates you're ready to strike. The longer the line you have out, the harder that is to do."

The streamers he likes best are the Black Ghost, the Muddler Minnow, and the Vamp. "The only place I've ever seen the Vamp described is in J. Edson Leonard's book *Flies*. I like a black-and-white streamer, and I use hackle wings instead of bucktail for the Vamp. I fish streamers mostly down and across, and I try to stay in contact visually. A lot of times while you're stripping the streamer in

and twitching it, there's a bit of slack there. A fish may be hitting and you're not going to feel it. But if you visually stay in contact, you'll see the fish take it."

Ed fishes everything from tiny mountain brooks to big freestone rivers. Although he does most of his fishing on the upper Beaverkill, his favorite stream is "the big river," the Delaware.

"In the Delaware, every fish has the potential to reach 20 inches. They're wild fish, rainbows over browns seven to one, and they'll take you into the backing on one run. If you fish two hours in the evening and get three fish, that's good. But I also love to catch little native brook trout in small mountain brooks. There are some big fish in those streams that would surprise you. Last week I was on a tributary of the Esopus, a little stream that nobody fishes, and there were browns up to 18 inches."

On occasion, Ed fishes with Lee Wulff. "Lee's not a match-the-hatch man," Ed says. He'll use a Royal Wulff, a hair-wing Royal Coachman, and an Adams. He kind of blows my mind. He's one of those guys who, if they're catching fish on an Adams, they'll change and try to find out what they can't catch them on.

"Lee will do that, but not me — I still want to catch every fish in the river!"

Greasing Up for Trout

by Reinhold Gatz

Using western steelhead techniques — distance casting and greased-line fishing — Russell Chatham has created a new approach for inland trout

"Stop the car!" Our guide's eyes gleamed with manic enthusiasm. "I see a fish!"

We were bouncing along the wrong side of a narrow dirt road that paralleled the winding course of the Oregon's North Umpqua River, braving an unexpected encounter with a redwood-heavy logging truck so Russell Chatham could study the flowing water below. John Bailey pulled off and parked. There was no guardrail, and the bank sloped precipitously to the river.

"There he is, by God!" Chatham rubbed his hands like Silas Marner contemplating a secret cache of gold.

Bailey and I stared down at the undulant surface of the Umpqua, seeing nothing but the dazzle of reflected sunlight. Chatham rummaged through the jumbled fishing tackle in the trunk, joining up a battered fiberglass rod. "Here." He handed me the rod as we scrambled down the steep bank. "You've never taken a steelhead. See that hump of water midstream? Cast above it. Quarter the stream, then mend your line as you retrieve."

I did as instructed, feeling like the sucker left holding the open sack on a midnight snipe hunt. On the second cast, I glanced to see if my companions were smirking. Chatham stared intently at the featureless surface of the river. Stripping in line, I felt a sudden jolt, as if I'd snagged a submerged log. "I'm hung up," I shrugged.

Chatham jumped up and down with glee. "You've got one on," he shouted, laughing like a madman.

Humpy dry fly skimmed across the surface with Russell Chatham's greased-line technique

Russell Chatham

Home: *Livingston, Montana*

Occupation: *Artist, writer*

As a boy in California, Russell Chatham fished almost every day of his life. During the school year, he'd be up before sunrise, fishing stripers in San Francisco Bay. And after the final-period bell rang, he'd be back at it for the rest of the afternoon. Vacations meant fishing from dawn to dark, seven days a week.

While still a teenager Chatham became an extraordinary distance fly caster, tutored by world casting champion Jon Tarrentino and other experts at the venerable Golden Gate Angling and Casting Club. This ability paid off on big coastal rivers such as the Klamath, Trinity, and Eel. "On those streams you had to cast a hundred feet to reach where the fish were," Chatham says. "Otherwise, you weren't going to catch anything."

He also learned to take large steelhead with the greased-line technique — first "greasing" his line, leader, and dry fly, then skimming them across the surface.

One of Chatham's most remarkable catches came on June 1966, in San Francisco Bay. On a fly of his own design, he caught a 36-pound 6-ounce striped bass — a fly-rod world record which was to stand for many years.

He's written scores of articles on fishing for such magazines as Sports Illustrated *and* The Atlantic. *His fishing books include* The Angler's Coast, Striped Bass on a Fly, Silent Seasons, *and* Dark Waters.

Chatham is a grandson of Gottardo Piazzoni, a noted California landscape artist and muralist. At age seven, Chatham started painting at the family ranch in Monterey County. Today, his landscapes are housed in museums and private collections around the world.

His recent projects include a magnificent series of lithographs, The Missouri Headwaters; *and the birth of a publishing venture, the Clark City Press, which will reprint his own books on fishing and bring out new poetry, fiction, and sporting literature.*

Chatham shoots out a long cast over a rising trout: his line flows perfectly smooth, no waves of slack

Then the steelhead started its run, the line racheting off the reel faster than my accelerating heartbeat.

I lost the fish. It threw the hook without ever coming into view. All the while, I wondered if Chatham had some sort of super-vision. How could he spot a rolling steelhead 200 feet away from a careening, jouncing car?

Over the next few days I observed other wonders: Chatham, his back against a bank thick with shrubby willow, roll-casting a lead-core shooting head 80 feet across the river to the deep channel along the opposite shore, where the fish were holding. He made it look easy, his rod describing a series of short arcs before letting the line rip.

Or the morning we fished the Steamboat Pool, made famous by Zane Grey decades earlier. Disciples of that long-dead master still roamed the cobbled river bend, elderly gentlemen with expensive custom rods and floppy "Zane Grey" hats. They were fishing dry flies and floating lines merely because that was the method preferred by the sainted Ohio dentist. They weren't catching any fish. The steelhead were down deep — stretched out in a wavering line on the bottom along the far bank, where the current surged against a wall of jagged boulders.

It was a hundred feet to this fish-choked slot. I was barely able to cast half that distance, and naturally came up empty-handed. Bailey, because of his insistence on using a delicate new 8-foot rod, dropped his fly 15 feet shy of the glory hole and caught only four or five stragglers. Chatham, with nothing behind him to impede his back cast, drove the heavy sinking line across the Umpqua, straight into the zone every time.

Within two hours, he landed and released seventeen steelhead. A group of Zane Grey clones gathered around to gawk in sullen disbelief.

Chatham has one stern dictum on fly fishing: He who casts farthest, casts best. Very few anglers can cast the full length of a fly line using their hands alone, no rod at all. Chatham is one of them. He double-hauls essentially the same as any good caster going for distance, but he does so with a timing and smoothness that seem uncanny. Besides an obvious aptitude, he has exceptional dedication, having spent literally thousands of hours practicing.

"In distance casting," he explains, "the line travels like a bullet coming out of a rifle. If you fire a bullet from a rifle and drop another bullet from the height of the muzzle at the same time, both bullets will hit the ground simultaneously. But one of them hits a mile away. The other one lands at your feet. Speed is distance. In order to achieve line speed in casting, you can't have any loose line. You can't have any slack between the rod tip and the unrolling loop. Your line must always be tight to the rod. To avoid putting slack in the line, every movement in the cast has to be perfectly smooth."

Searching for cheaper rents and horizons broader than the Disneyland vistas of modern California, Chatham moved to Montana in 1972. He now lives on the banks of the hallowed Yellowstone River, in Livingston. Other world-famous trout streams such as the Madison, Gallatin, and Big Hole lie within easy driving distance.

Years of steelhead fishing are the secret weapon he brings to mountain trout angling. The fall after he moved to Montana, he found his shooting head and distance casting remarkably effective in driving big streamers across the Yellowstone for spawning browns. He also found that his greased-line technique worked as well for Rocky Mountain trout as it did for steelhead.

There's no such thing as an all-purpose dry-fly method, but Chatham's greased-line technique comes as close as any. Dry flies are generally less versatile than nymphs and streamers. They produce excellent fishing during a hatch, provided you can figure out which of the insect species on the water the trout are grabbing, and provided you can drift your imitation past a feeding fish with no trace of drag. But when nothing is hatching and the water seems barren of trout, a dry fly cast to all the likely spots and dead-drifted to perfection will often get you blisters on your casting hand, and not much more.

In this technique the fly is not allowed to drift passively but is actually retrieved across the water: if the line tip starts to go under, the leader and fly won't be far behind. To ensure that everything stays on top, Chatham greases it — "grease" being the term from steelhead fishing for paste floatant. He rubs the paste onto the front portion of his line, the entire length of his leader, and then — sparingly — onto the hackle, tail, and hair body of his fly.

Chatham's aim is to suggest a natural insect skimming along the surface. The natural could be a caddis or mayfly or almost any other aquatic species. It might be struggling to get airborne during a hatch, or it might simply be blowing along the surface at the whim of the breeze.

A variety of dry-fly patterns will serve the purpose, Chatham says. "The Elk Hair Caddis is good. So are the Humpy types and the Irresistible. Buoyant flies, bushy stuff that stays up on the surface. The exact pattern isn't very important, just the visibility and floatability. I like the Elk Hair Caddis with the light hair and the upturned front. Sixteen seems the optimum size, but once in a while I'll use something one size bigger."

Chatham has a healthy ironic suspicion of the equipment mania gripping the fly-fishing fraternity. In the not-so-distant past, he made do with ancient battered rods held together with peeling electrician's tape. He doesn't wear a vest crammed with exotic and costly doodads; in fact, he doesn't wear a vest at all. He prefers to carry a canvas bag

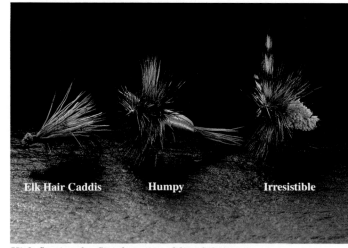

High-floating dry flies for greased-line fishing

Keeping it simple: Chatham's fishing kit

filled with whatever lines, leaders, and flies he might need for a day's fishing.

The rods he likes for greased-lining run from 3- to 6-weight — the latter only for larger waters like the Yellowstone. Lengths from 8 to 9 feet are ideal; the extra-long graphite models many anglers now buy for delicate dry-fly fishing aren't necessary. Nearly all his reels are vintage Pflueger Medalists — very rugged, though heavier than most of the newer reels. "I don't care about the weight," he says. "The heavier reel makes the rod seem lighter. It moves the balance point back. Those older Medalists are the best reels ever made. I just like them better."

Either double-taper or weight-forward floating lines will do the job. He uses long leaders: "I like to keep it out there 12 feet at least." The tippet weight varies, but 5X is his usual choice for size 16 flies.

If trout are rising, he casts well ahead of a rise. The cast may be aimed upstream, across, or down — whatever it takes to reach a fish. Ideally, Chatham likes to get in position for a cast across stream, then let the fly swing on the current. On lakes, he tries to determine the course of an individual fish as it moves along just beneath the surface and rises at intervals. He figures where it's headed and casts so the fly will be waiting when it arrives. "If there's no activity on the surface, then you can cast blind and that works very well. Of course if you do see something, you can be more focused in. Most days you do a little of each."

Getting the retrieve right is the key. Chatham generally keeps his rod tip close to the water, and works

the fly back in short, continuous strips. Each strip is about 4 or 5 inches long. The fly skims across the surface in stop-and-go fashion, trailing a diminutive wake. Fished this way, a fly calls more attention to itself than one drifted dead on the surface. "That's exactly how you fish dry for steelhead," says Chatham. "Just hang it in the current, then skim it across."

This differs from a more common — and less widely useful — method of skating a dry fly. In that way of doing it, the fly must be cast downstream, then the rod tip must be held high while the line is stripped in. The fly tends to bounce rather than skim. It's effective, but far more limited in value. The rod must be long and the line very light, a 5-weight at most; the casts must be kept short, and you can't fish across stream or upstream.

"If you get everything greased," says Chatham, "you don't need to hold the rod tip high. When you're casting across stream and letting the fly swing down, then you might want to hold the tip up a little to reduce the line belly on the water. And you can cast as far as you want — a hundred feet — and still make the fly move the way it has to." His method works equally well for wading, or float-tubing, or casting to the streambanks from a drift boat.

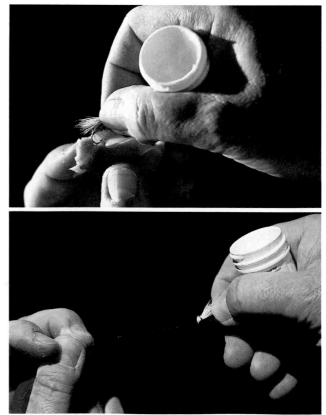

Fly and leader get a dab of ''grease''

134

When a trout rises to the fly, Chatham is careful not to strike too soon, before the fish really has it. "I prefer to let an instant elapse. Also, with a 5X tippet you don't want to strike too hard. There's a certain amount of drag on the line that helps set the hook."

Chatham would be the last to lay claim to any complex tactics of the sort that fly-fishing magazines and books now offer as standard fare. He's merely taken an approach proven in one kind of fishing, and adapted it to another. Nor would he say he's the only one who's done so. "I pretty much worked it out on my own, but subsequently I've seen some explanations by others of more or less the same thing."

His greased-line trick catches fish all during the trout season, spring through fall. It doesn't require any specific combination of water and weather conditions for success; it works on lakes and on streams. There's no special time of day that's best. Nor is it limited to any one hatch, or to hatches in general.

"If there's nothing going on," says Chatham, "you're creating an interest. It's an attractor type of activity. Often it works when other methods won't." Even in a strong wind, the spoiler of ordinary dry-fly fishing, it's "terrific, absolutely — the rougher it gets, the better it works."

Not that it *always* takes fish. On spring creeks, it "will work sometimes, but not consistently." These waters are shallow and very clear, and on days with no wind to stir the surface and no trout moving at all, the greased line won't perform any miracles. "If it's dead calm on a spring creek, I think it just scares them."

Recently, Chatham heard some reports of big trout being taken from Len's Lake in the Paradise Valley south of Livingston. So he loaded up a new float tube and decided to give the small lake a try. He brought along a gleaming new 8½-foot Sage rod, a 3-weight, and one of his weathered antique Medalists. He looked appropriately ridiculous in latex waders and the float tube, not a device designed with dignity as its primary function. He duck-waddled into the lake on the ungainly flippers, his eyes rolled heavenward in mock despair. "The advantage of the tube," he was quick to point out, "is it doesn't make any noise like wading. You can move right along with the fish."

Not long after he started, however, an enormous wind blew up, as suddenly as if God had flipped some cosmic power switch. The dead calm reflection of the Absaroka Range was erased with a corrugated rush of whitecaps. Back on shore, Chatham

Chatham releases handsome rainbow at Len's Lake

discarded the useless float tube and scanned the surface of Len's Lake. The conditions were such that a lesser angler would immediately have headed for the saloon.

He grinned defiantly, stripping line in a powerful double haul and driving his cast in a tight loop straight into the teeth of the wind. He retrieved the Elk Hair Caddis with sharp tugs, making it skim erratically over the waves — a far cry from delicate chalk-stream finesse. The grease kept his fly and leader floating high on the choppy surface.

The results were immediate. A rise; then the water boiled as a large trout cartwheeled into the air. After a brief but powerful struggle, Chatham coaxed an iridescent 3½-pound rainbow into the shallows.

Although he'd performed this act thousands of times, he beamed like a kid with his first trophy as he slipped the barbless hook from the upper jaw of the trout, then eased it back into the water.

Trout & Salmon Tips

Brian Cummings
Split-Shot on Spinner Shafts

Spinners such as the Luhr Jensen Skagit Special and Tee-Spoon draw lots of strikes from king salmon, but the problem is to get the lures deep enough to be effective. Kings tend to move into rivers during periods of high water — late spring and early summer in Alaska — and usually hug the bottom in current. The large blades of the Skagit and Tee-Spoon have lots of attractive flash, but their water resistance keeps them from reaching bottom in deep holes with swift flow. Brian Cummings, a guide who lives in Anchorage and fishes the Nushagak River in southwest Alaska, removes some of the plastic beads from the lures and replaces them with split-shot. Not only do the lures track much deeper, but they cast much better so you can reach way out in big pools. Retrieve slowly so the spinner bumps along the bottom. One word of caution: lures with shot added may not be allowed in some places, because of regulations intended to halt salmon-snagging.

SELECT a Skagit or Tee-Spoon with a size 5 or 6 blade. Using electrician's cutters, snip one or two of the large plastic beads, and remove. Replace with split-shot.

Kris Hollmer
Tickler for Streamers

In high, discolored water, a small spinner blade attached to the hook of a streamer will help attract fish. Kris Hollmer, a fishing and hunting guide from Red Bluff, California, calls the blade a "tickler" and says it works especially well for coho salmon and brown trout. In fast water, the current will make the spinner blade flutter; in slower water, working the fly with a twitching action will make the blade flash.

PINCH the hook barb down, then slip a barrel swivel attached to a split-ring and spinner blade onto the bend. Use a paper punch to cut a tab from a plastic lid; press the tab over the hook to keep the swivel from slipping off. A streamer with a long-shank hook and a wing that does not extend beyond the hook bend works best.

Aaron Richardson
Salmon-Egg Keeper

Aaron Richardson, a salesman for a sporting-goods store in Missoula, Montana, uses a piece of surgical tubing to keep an egg sac firmly in place on a hook. Richardson fishes for big steelhead and salmon in the rivers of Idaho, and for a long time he was annoyed by the egg-angler's bugaboo: his spawn sac would be left barely hanging from the hook after a few casts, so he'd have to re-rig. The surgical-tubing keeper saves him time and eggs alike, and holds better than a piece of rubber band or a plastic tab.

SNIP off a ¼-inch length of surgical tubing, then cut this into crescent-shaped halves. After attaching a spawn sac to an egg hook, pierce one of these halves with the hook and slide it up the bend until its concave side is snug against the sac.

Trout Tips from Bob White
Suck Leech Fly

Many Alaska guides, including White, are using an unusually effective new fly pattern intended to simulate a leech carrying a salmon egg in its mouth. White says that big trout in coastal streams will often watch a leech taking an egg from a salmon redd, then take leech and egg with one gulp. One big advantage of this pattern is that it rarely hooks a trout deeply; ordinary egg flies often are swallowed instantly, and the trout may not survive after it is released.

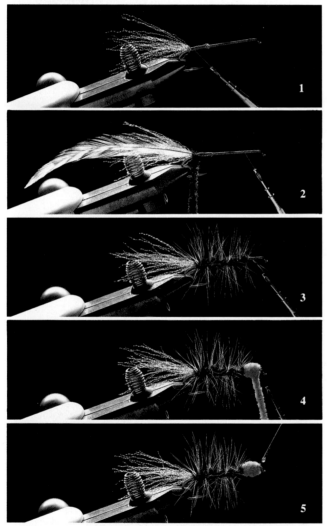

TIE a Suck Leech by (1) wrapping tying thread along two-thirds of the shank of a long-shank hook, size 4 to 8; lead wire may also be wound on, for a faster sink rate. Tie in a tail of Krystal Flash or black marabou. (2) Tie on a length of black or dark olive chenille, and a soft grizzly hackle feather. Wind the thread to a point near the eye, then wrap the chenille up to the eye and tie off. (3) Wrap the hackle around the chenille and tie off. (4) Tie in a length of peach, orange, red, or chartreuse chenille, and wrap it thick to form the egg. (5) Tie off at the eye, and seal the windings of thread with waterproof cement.

BOB WHITE, whose official hometown is Minneapolis, guides fly fishermen in Alaska and Argentina most of the year. He's caught countless trophy trout over 8 pounds, and *Rod & Reel* magazine presented him its Guide of the Year award in 1988.

Leader Sleeves for Fishing Deeper

White uses sliding brass sleeves on his fly leaders, instead of split-shot. The sleeves are manufactured for use with downrigger equipment and wire leaders. Tiny shot spread along a leader do a good job of getting flies deep in current, but they're hard to cast and a nuisance to attach, usually dropping into the stream before you can squeeze them shut. And they tend to work loose during casting. In contrast, the sleeves thread onto the leader and can't come off unless the leader breaks. They are light and streamlined, so they cast easily. Another advantage: because they slide freely on the leader, they work like a slip-sinker. When a fish grabs the fly, it feels less resistance than it would with split-shot.

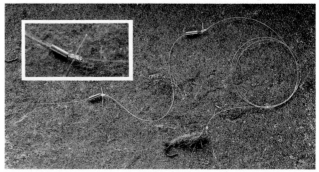

SLIDE one sleeve on each leader section when tying a knotted leader. Knotless leaders can be cut at several points, and then retied after the sleeves are installed. Leave stubs on your blood knots, so the sleeves can't slip from section to section.

Striped Bass, Catfish & Mixed-Bag Saltwater

Mixed Bag in Belize

by Dick Sternberg

Charles Westby demonstrates the light-tackle techniques that make him one of the Caribbean's most versatile fishing guides

After months of staring through a hole in the ice, northern anglers start dreaming of warmer climes and open water — places like the Florida Keys, the Bahamas, and Central America.

In the middle of a recent February, I flew from Minnesota to spend ten days with guide Charles Westby on a variety-pack fishing trip in Belize. Also heading south to defrost were photographer Bill Lindner of the *Hunting and Fishing Library,*

and Larry Dahlberg and Jim Lindner of the *In-Fisherman* television series. Our goal: to go after as many different Belizean fish as possible — blue-water, channel, reef, and flats species — and discover some of Westby's secrets for catching them.

At first, Charlie seemed somewhat reserved — not the type that was going to volunteer much information. But he answered every question without hesitation, and in his matter-of-fact style, outlined his strategy for each species. I knew that he specialized in fishing the flats, but I was surprised to find that he had extensive knowledge of nearly every sport fish that inhabits Belizean waters, including blue-water and river species. We spent most of our time chasing bonefish, wahoo and snook.

Charles Westby

Home: *Crooked Tree Village, Belize*

Occupation: *Fishing guide operating out of Sail Belize on Moho Cay, Belize City*

Considering how Charles Westby spent his boyhood, it's no wonder he has gained a reputation as one of Central America's top fishing guides. Charlie's father and grandfather made their livings as commercial fishermen. They dived for lobster and conch,

and spearfished and handlined along the Belize barrier reef, which is second in size only to Australia's barrier reef. Charlie and his three brothers learned about fish and fishing from their elders, and Charlie's brothers continue the family's commercial-fishing tradition.

After Charlie's father became the head lighthouse-keeper in Belize, frequent inspection trips took him to all the lighthouses along the reef. Charlie tagged along on many of these trips, becoming familiar with many different sections of the reef. The waters around the reef offered Charlie an excellent training ground in his quest to become a successful guide. Bonefish, snook, tarpon, and permit cruise the flats in amazing numbers; giant grouper prowl the edges of the reef; and wahoo, kingfish, blue and white marlin, and sailfish abound in the blue water.

Westby with a 30-pound yellowfin grouper, a common Caribbean reef species

Westby keeps low when casting to tailing bonefish

Bonefish

We were plagued by cold, rainy weather for the first few days of our trip. Under cold-front conditions, bonefish move to deeper water off the edge of the flats, where they may be tough to find. Charlie likes to fish for them on a sunny day following such a front. Then you can see them tailing on the flats as they root around for small crabs.

When the sun finally broke through, we decided to try one of Charlie's favorite flats around Turneffe Island, a world-famous bonefishing area. The Turneffe flats, unlike those closer to the mainland, have a hard sand bottom ideal for wading.

It was about 11 a.m. when we pulled our boat up to the edge of the flat. We anchored, then jumped into the water wearing shorts and tennis shoes. I was eager to catch a bonefish on a fly, so we started walking down the flat, looking for tailing fish. Less than a hundred yards from the boat Charlie stopped abruptly, and without uttering a word pointed ahead. At first, I couldn't see what he was looking at, but then I spotted a half-dozen nearly transparent tails: a school of feeding bones.

Charlie gestured to follow him, and we worked our way upwind of the school, staying as low as possible. I later learned that bones move into the wind to feed, and by getting upwind you don't have to cast over their heads and risk spooking them.

After getting into position, I dropped the fly just ahead of the school and started stripping line in 6-inch jerks. A bone struck almost instantly. All I could do was hold on as the fish peeled off all the fly line and a good portion of the backing. Finally it stopped running, I gained some line, and soon I was admiring my first fly-rod bone, a brilliant, silvery 5-pounder.

On Charlie's advice, I was using an 8½-foot fly rod, a WF8F line, and a 6-foot tapered leader with an 8-pound tippet. Charlie prefers flies smaller

A collection of bonefish flies tied by Westby

than normal; bonefish often cruise in water only a foot deep, and smaller flies sink more slowly and hang up in the turtle grass less often. His theory on color selection: "Use a fly the color of the bottom. Most natural foods camouflage themselves to match their surroundings."

We continued down the flat, and Charlie spotted school after school of bonefish, some as far as 150 yards ahead. When asked how he could spot them so far away, he replied, "Look for a flash." He was spotting glints of light that I mistook for rippling water. After he pointed out exactly what to look for, I was able to spot the fish too, but never as well as he could.

After landing a couple more bones, we spotted another school. These fish, however, were cruising rather than tailing. I cast in their direction, but just as the fly was about to alight, the water exploded and the fish were gone.

"They're done feeding," Charlie said. "Tide's out and fishing's gonna be tough."

We saw several more schools, but each one spooked before the fly hit the water. The pattern was just as Charlie had predicted. He prefers to fish before 10:30 a.m. or after 2 p.m., preferably on an incoming or outgoing tide. At low tide, the fish become spooky and move to the deep edge of the reef.

We fished bones several other times over the course of the trip, and each time Charlie quickly found the fish. They weren't huge, but there were always plenty of them.

Wahoo

Even though Charlie specializes in fishing the flats, he has a hard time ignoring the excellent blue-water fishing off Belize. Of all the blue-water species, his favorite is the wahoo. And no wonder. Some knowledgeable anglers say Belize's wahoo fishing is the world's best.

Wahoo spawn from October into December, and that's when fishing is hot. February finds wahoo action on a steep downhill slide, so I wondered whether we should spend our time on something else. "We'll catch wahoo," Charlie assured me in his typical calm, confident tone. "All we need is a sunny day. The fish see the baits better then."

In bright weather we headed for Glory Caye, one of Charlie's most reliable wahoo spots. Along the way, we were rigging leaders and trolling baits on our lines when Charlie abruptly turned the wheel.

"Frigate birds. Might be a school of tuna," he speculated. "Put on feathers."

We snapped trolling feathers onto two of the lines and quickly let them out. Some distance before we reached the diving birds, both rods jumped. Billy and I grabbed the rods, and line began singing from the reels. From the power of the run, I guessed my fish would go 50 pounds, but I finally landed a bigeye tuna of no more than 12. The tuna's streamlined shape makes it a swimming machine, and its power is astounding. Billy landed one about the same size.

Dahlberg lands a "bone" as Westby poles the skiff

Westby uses a 26-foot Shamrock to fish the blue water

143

We reset the lines, and almost immediately another pair struck. The frenzy lasted only ten minutes, but we boated eight bigeyes and missed several more. Then the school sounded and we resumed our wahoo hunt.

Charlie suggested we cut one of the tuna into strips for tipping our wahoo lures. Strip bait isn't necessary when the fish are biting, but it helps when fishing is slow. Charlie prefers skirted plastic trolling lures in blue, green, purple, orange, or some combination of these. He recommends a trailer hook, because wahoo tend to strike short. But the 8-inch strip bait should be pushed over the leading hook only.

When we arrived at Glory Caye, Charlie showed us a long point jutting into the blue water, a natural wahoo magnet. His strategy was to troll around the point, keeping the boat about a quarter mile out in the blue water, which meant we were fishing over 100- to 200-foot depths. His trolling speed was very fast — about 8 miles per hour. At this speed, the plastic lures skipped enticingly along the surface. "Can't troll too fast for wahoo," Charlie explained. My fish books proved him to be right. A wahoo swims at speeds up to 45 mph. A steelhead, the fastest fish known to freshwater anglers, can swim only 21 mph.

To avoid spooking the wahoo, Charlie steered the boat in S-curves. This way, the lures passed over

S-trolling for wahoo

undisturbed water, rather than following in the wake of the boat. He also used outriggers to keep some of the lures to the side.

The action was slow for the first couple of hours. Then suddenly there was a swirl behind one of the baits, and Charlie yelled *"wa-hoooo"* as a long, sleek fish rocketed high into the air. Now I know how the species got its name. A wahoo's first leap literally takes your breath away. It can easily clear the water by 10 feet, and may jump much higher.

I grabbed the rod and watched helplessly as the 50-pound mono melted off the reel. After two more jumps the fish started to tire, and ten minutes later we had our first wahoo, a beautiful 40-pounder. When we first hauled it aboard, its coloration was spectacular — iridescent purplish blue sides with

Westby and Sternberg with 40-pound wahoo

dark vertical bars. But in minutes the color faded to a dull gray.

Before we got the fish unhooked, Charlie pivoted the boat and headed back where the wahoo hit. We had only two lines in the water, but a few seconds after we reached the spot a fish struck. This one was smaller, about 30 pounds, and Billy subdued it quickly.

In the next half hour, three more wahoo took swipes at the lures but missed. Then something grabbed the biggest plastic bait and took off in the opposite direction. The fish was pulling so hard that I could barely get the rod out of the holder. It finally slowed down and began a tug-of-war. All I could do was hold on as line clicked slowly off the reel. Fifteen minutes later, the fish made a run for the surface. I reeled as fast as I could to take up the slack, but there was no hope. The fish was gone.

"Big wahoo," Charlie surmised. "Eighty- or ninety-pounder."

We continued fishing, but the school either moved or stopped feeding. Charlie explained that the fast bite we had enjoyed corresponded to a tide change. Wahoo usually feed heavily at the turn of the tide, either incoming or outgoing. The lesson is that you've got to move quickly, to get in on the bite while it lasts.

How to Cut and Rig Tuna Strips

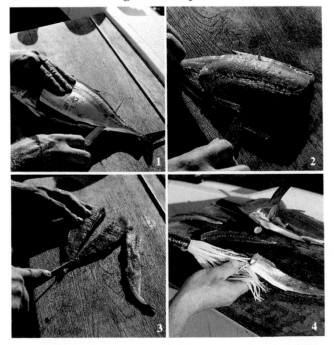

(1) Cut fillets from both sides of tuna. (2) Slice each fillet horizontally to reduce thickness. (3) Cut skin-on fillet lengthwise into 1-inch strips. (4) Push front hook through wide end of tuna strip.

Snook

Normally, snook are easy to catch in rivers in February, but Charlie explained that the recent heavy rains had muddied the water so much that the snook couldn't see the bait. The best bet would be to work the same flats where we had been catching bonefish.

Snook spend most of the day tucked under mangrove roots. They come out to feed at night. Charlie says you may find them cruising the edge of the mangroves at dawn and again at dusk, or when the tide starts to rise.

Snook find excellent cover in the mangrove roots

When they're tucked into the roots, you may be able to squeeze a fly beneath the overhang, if you're a good fly caster. Otherwise, you're better off casting surface plugs when they're out feeding. For fly casting, Charlie recommended a 9-weight rod with a weight-forward line. To keep the line from fouling on the mangrove limbs, he advised holding the rod parallel to the surface and side-casting.

Charlie quietly poled the boat along the edge of the mangroves, peering beneath the limbs for any sign of snook. Larry stood at the bow, ready to cast. The reflections on the surface made the fish difficult to see, even with polarized glasses, but Charlie had no trouble spotting them. "Big school," he whispered, pointing to a dark hole beneath a clump of protruding mangroves.

Larry, an expert fly caster, placed his streamer right on the mark and began stripping line in sharp

At dusk, snook move out of the mangroves and cruise the flats

jerks. Three snook appeared from beneath the branches, eyes glued to the darting fly.

"Strip, strip, strip," Charlie urged, and Larry did just that.

A snook grabbed the fly, made a quick turn and headed for the mangrove roots. But Larry snubbed it down and managed to keep it in open water. Snook are explosive fighters, and this one was no exception. After several powerful runs, Larry finally boated the fish — a chunky 6-pounder.

Dahlberg with a 6-pound snook that hit a streamer

"Snook won't hit the fly if you stop stripping," Charlie explained. "Make them think the fly's getting away from them." This tip paid off not only for snook, but also for bonefish, tarpon, barracuda, and practically every other species that roams the flats.

Most of the snook we caught were in the 4- to 8-pound class. There were plenty of bigger ones around, but they were much warier and not as

active during the day. Charlie catches the big ones in early morning, until first light, then gets them again at dusk. Many of the biggest snook are caught at night. After dark, they cruise the flats and are easy to catch on noisy surface plugs like the Creek Chub Darter, Nip-I-Diddee, and Dalton Special. For

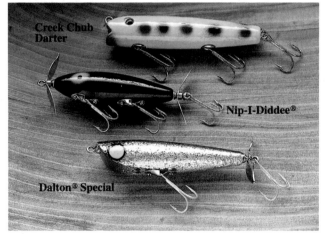

Westby's favorite topwater snook plugs

plug fishing, Charlie uses a 7-foot flipping stick and a baitcasting reel spooled with 14-pound mono. Snook have raspy teeth, so he uses a foot-long tippet of 80-pound mono.

During our trip, Charlie did very little fishing himself, opting instead to run the boat, look for fish, and give us advice on how to catch them. Besides the species already mentioned, he showed us some excellent fishing for grouper, king mackerel, and barracuda. Time ran out before we had a chance to fish for permit, one of his specialties.

What impressed me most about Charlie was that he had developed his fishing skills in a region practically devoid of modern sportfishing technology. Not only that, but the area is practically devoid of other fishermen as well, except for native handliners. You can't help admiring a guy who's made it on his own.

A Gallery of Belizean Sportfish

Westby and Sternberg with bigeye tuna

Lindner with barracuda

Dahlberg with tarpon

Lindner with black grouper; Dahlberg with cubera snapper

Westby and Lindner with king mackerel

Cats That Ain't Kittens

by Gerald Almy

Using his cut-bait technique, Captain John Sellers has probably boated more giant catfish than anyone else in North America

It's a warm Indian-summer day on 60,000-acre Lake Moultrie, the smaller of two sprawling impoundments that make up Santee-Cooper's 170,000 acres of fish-filled water. Thick mats of pewter-colored clouds block out the sun. A light wind blows the gray-green waters in a slapping drumbeat against the hull of John Sellers' boat.

Sellers grabs a fresh gizzard shad from the cooler, cuts off the head, slices the body into five ¾-inch steaks, then discards the tail. He impales the steaks and the head on 5/0 hooks. He strips line from his reels in carefully measured increments, then places the rods into sturdy, black iron holders, so the tips point parallel to the water and are just a few feet above it.

And now it's a waiting game — waiting and watching the rod tips, as we drift along rough bottom structure in 30 feet of water. The baits dangle just inches off the bottom. We pass over an old canal 40 feet down, dug by slaves to connect the Santee and Cooper rivers long before the famous lakes were formed half a century ago. Sitting back, we study the rods intently from the padded seats of the 22-foot Citation — once white, now with a tannish cast from the slime and grit of years of catfishing.

Though Santee-Cooper is the birthplace of fresh-water striper fishing, and is renowned for cypress-loving largemouths up to 16 pounds and world-class crappies up to 5, the undisputed king of this huge pair of lakes is the catfish. And no wonder. What other fish can you go after in fresh water with a realistic chance of catching a 40-, 50-, even 60-pounder? Fish like that are a distinct possibility every day at Santee-Cooper. Cats now draw more interest than any other species on the lakes, thanks in large part to the tremendous catches made by "Big John" Sellers — a man who's 5½ feet of solid catfishing legend.

At the age of 22, Sellers became a full-time guide on Santee-Cooper. The lakes were young then, and channel cats, largemouth bass, and stripers were the main gamefish. When flatheads were added to the lake, and then blue catfish, John found himself catching bigger and bigger cats each season.

Although Sellers still guides for striped bass, the catfish is his first choice. Stripers run 5 to 15 pounds in the lakes; blue cats in the better spots average 10 to 25 pounds, with the chance of a 30- to 60-pounder ever present. The lake record is 86 pounds, and John has a hunch there are cats here that would top the century mark.

Sellers is a quiet, gentle man who in his own way — with action rather than talk — has promoted the

---

John Sellers

Home: *Cross, South Carolina*

Occupation: *Catfish and striped bass guide*

Catching a 50-pound fish in fresh water is a pinnacle that few anglers ever reach. But for John Sellers, landing one that size or better is almost a weekly occurrence. He guides for giant blue, flathead, and channel catfish on the Santee-Cooper lakes in central South Carolina.

He's been a catfish fan since he first caught them as a youngster in the small tannin-stained creeks near his home. The Santee-Cooper lakes were formed in the early 1940s, and Sellers started guiding on these waters for catfish and stripers about ten years later. Since then, he has established a reputation as one of the finest catfishermen not only in the South, but in the entire country.

Sellers won two of the first major catfishing contests held on Santee-Cooper. In the first, he amassed a single-day winning catch of 263 pounds to win the total weight division, and his largest cat, a 54-pounder, took big-fish honors. During a single year, anglers guided by Sellers took 100 catfish weighing over 50 pounds. His top blue cat so far is a 64-pounder, and top flathead 49 pounds. On one incredible day, a single client from North Carolina caught five catfish weighing from 53 to 59 pounds.

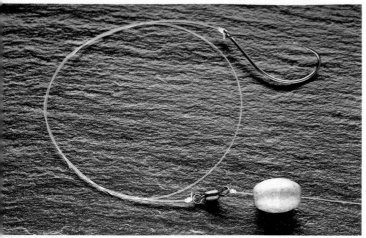

TIE size 4/0 to 6/0 hook to 18-inch, 50-pound mono leader; add barrel swivel to other end. Thread ½- to 2-ounce egg sinker onto 30-pound mono line; tie to swivel.

SLICE a large gizzard shad (shown), threadfin shad, mullet, or blueback herring into steaks ¾ inch wide. Only steaks and head are used as bait.

HOOK the head lightly through the snout. The steaks (not shown) are hooked in the belly, through one side and out the other.

sport and challenge of trophy catfishing. His catches speak louder than any sales pitch could. Calmly, without boasting, he has rewritten the record books on the number of 50-pound fish one guide has accounted for — he's also rewritten the how-to manuals on fooling giant cats. In this rural area where fishing and hunting are the main topics of conversation at roadside diners, Sellers has become something of a hero.

Once, in a single day, Sellers' clients came in with thirteen huge catfish. Their total weight? Four hundred and thirty-seven pounds.

The two anglers aboard today don't have their sights set quite so high. They do, however, hope they can latch onto at least a single trophy cat. Sharon Taylor has come 750 miles from New York to fish for her favorite quarry; I've traveled 500 miles from Virginia.

Hearteningly, the cats are there. Using his depth finder, Sellers locates appropriate structure — "anything rough or broken, or covered with stumps, or dropping off sharply" — then pinpoints fish holding near the lake floor. We can see them clearly on Sellers' Si-Tex LCR, hovering like huge logs just off the bottom.

Sellers begins a drift. "If the big cats are around," he says, "you can usually see them easily on the depth finder. The only exception is when it's real windy and rough. Then they're harder to see. They just kind of blend into the bottom."

He has dozens of favorite catfish locations on the lakes, discovered in endless hours of studying topographical maps, motoring around the lake with a depth finder, then test-fishing. Among these spots are hills, dropoffs, saddles, edges of creek channels, ditches, submerged islands, holes on an otherwise flat bottom, flooded bridges, roadbeds, sunken canals and building foundations. All are good structure and cover for blue cats. Occasionally he also fishes fields of dead standing timber, especially for flatheads.

The depth we're fishing now is 34 feet — a typical level in midday fishing for cats, according to John. "Early in the day and late in the evening the fish move shallower. I sometimes fish in as little as 8 or 10 feet of water in the morning or at dusk. The big ones often move in then to feed on flats, bars, points, and shallow humps. During the middle of the day like this, though, they hang deeper, 20 to 60 feet, around rough cover.

"Whatever depth you're fishing, it's important to keep your bait within inches of the bottom. I use anywhere from ½ to 2 ounces of lead, and let line out whenever necessary during the drift to make sure the bait stays close to the bottom. You'll get hung up some. That's just part of the game if you want to catch big cats."

A rod bounces with a sharp tapping in its holder. The two anglers jump to their feet, wondering if they should grab the rod and pay out line to the fish, or go ahead and strike.

"No need for that," Sellers says calmly. "I don't fish for little cats. I use big baits and big hooks so the small ones can't take them. We catch a few tykes, but most of the fish you see bobbing the rod lightly like that are just youngsters that can't get the big chunks of shad or mullet in their mouths.

"When a nice cat takes, you'll know it. They strike like a bolt of lightning. The rod jerks down hard and stays down. Sometimes the tip buries itself in the water. They hook themselves. I've never seen a fish in fresh water that strikes as violently as a big blue cat."

Sellers has actually had cats that were hooked in the shallows leap clear of the water like a largemouth or tarpon. Expect your heart to creep into your throat a bit when a 30-pound blue does that.

As we drift into the channel of the old canal, Sellers releases line from the reels so the baits stay on the bottom. Soon a tenacious 3-pounder scarfs down a chunk of cut mullet and holds on until it hooks itself. The fish is cranked in unceremoniously, and Sellers quickly twists the hook free and releases it unharmed — a potential trophy cat.

"I've tried fishing at night," he goes on, "but they don't seem to bite any better then. Big cats feed during the day as well as at night. You just have to know where they hang out, what they want to eat, and how to present it to them. Another thing — when you hook into a 50-pounder, he's a lot easier to deal with in daylight than at night. Big cats are going to feed an hour or two every day. The trick is to put a bait in front of them when that feed period occurs. It might be early in the day, late, or high noon."

Drifting is another of Sellers' secrets for catching giant cats. Most fishermen believe you have to anchor and wait for cats, letting a scent trail slither out in the current and waft its odor to the whiskered quarry. Keep the bait in place, goes the adage, so the slow, lazy fish can find and eat it. Sellers knows that big trophy cats are far more aggressive and faster than this. They can easily nab a bait that's drifting across the bottom, and do not hesitate to do so.

Only an hour into the afternoon, we've already swept across hundreds of yards of prime bottom

Sellers uses 9-foot graphite rods, heavy level-wind reels

How to Drift-Fish with Cut Bait

PLACE rods in holders after lowering baits to a few inches from bottom. As you drift, watch rod tips for bites and check your sonar for changes in bottom depth.

ADJUST line length quickly when depth changes, to keep baits in fish zone and minimize snagging. Reel in periodically to check baits for debris or to add fresh bait.

contour, dragging six tempting baits that can attract cats with their scent as well as movement. "By drifting, I cover a lot more water and actually search for fish. Instead of waiting for the cats to come to me, I go to them."

There are times when Sellers will anchor: when the fish are less active in midwinter, when the wind is so strong that the boat rocks violently and it's hard to control the baits, or when the cats are in the shallows in March and April. "Big cats might be in as little as 3 to 5 feet of water in spring, because the shallow water warms more quickly than the depths. For drifting, there are too many stumps and snags to get hung up on, and you're likely to spook the fish if your boat goes over them in water that thin." Anchoring and casting up onto prime feeding areas such as bars, points, and humps is more effective.

Another myth John refutes is that big cats can only be caught on putrid blood or cheese concoctions, stink baits, or rotten fish. These baits are best for channel cats, but blues and flatheads prefer fresh fish. "You don't need a rotten, smelly offering to attract big cats," says Sellers. "They're used to feeding on other fish, usually live ones. They're a clean, strong sport fish. They're not garbage eaters."

Sellers uses fresh fish whenever possible; the rest of the time, he settles for the freshest frozen fish he can find. The best bait varies with the season. Whole threadfin shad are good during the winter months. Later, from mid-February into April, blueback herring are by far the top offering. These slender, oily, anadromous fish swarm up the Cooper River on their spawning run during this period. They get into the lakes via a lift at the dam at Moncks Corner. Sellers catches his herring below the dam with a cast net; sometimes he freezes an extra supply for later use.

By summer, cut gizzard shad becomes the prime offering. Sellers catches these baitfish at night in the canal between lakes Marion and Moultrie. He attracts them with lights and then hurls a cast net. Cut mullet, frozen or fresh, are equally effective. Cut sections of bluegills, or whole small ones, will work in a pinch.

Whichever bait he settles on, Sellers likes a sturdy, wide-gap hook such as the Eagle Claw Series 42. He uses a 50-pound mono leader, and a ½- to 2-ounce egg sinker. His 9-foot graphite rods are medium-heavy; the heavy-duty level-wind reels are spooled with 30-pound mono. It's sporting tackle, yet strong enough to handle fish in the 30- to 60-pound class, when used properly.

Sellers struggles to hoist 53-pound blue cat

At 3:30 p.m., that tackle gets a chance to show its stuff. A heavy fish nails a bait and Sharon Taylor grabs the rod. The big cat comes up grudgingly after ten minutes of stubborn fighting. Sellers gets ready with the long-handled net, but the cat wallows and thrashes just out of reach, astounding the anglers with its size. Then the monster dives deep again and slugs it out for another ten minutes.

"You rarely get them the first time they come up," says Sellers, reassuringly. "About twenty minutes — that's what it usually takes to get a big one in. He's giving up some bubbles from his air bladder now. That should mean he's about ready."

The long rod provides leverage to keep the cat away from the boat as it struggles to dive under the motor. Finally, 25 minutes after hookup, the grueling battle comes to an end. Taylor pumps the fish to the surface and the net enmeshes it. Hoisting hard, Sellers pulls in a 53-pounder. After photos, it's wrestled into the stash box in the front deck. Even when the fish is curled up, its tail sticks out — like the antlers of a trophy buck peeking out above a pickup truck's bed. And it is every bit as much a trophy.

The wind is rising now, kicking up out of the east at 10 to 15 knots. Sellers shakes his head disappointedly. "Strong wind is the worst thing in the world for this type of fishing. A light wind, almost calm, is best. When the wind kicks up, it stirs up the big cats and they move around a lot more, so they're harder to pinpoint. It also rocks the boat so much that the baits constantly bob up and down 2 or 3 feet. That makes it harder for the cats to connect when they strike.'' The best bet, according to Sellers, is to head for the lee side of the lake, where the water is calmer.

Unfortunately, the spots that have been producing best of late are on the windward side. So we stick it out, rocking and bouncing, hoping the baits are not moving too much to entice the cats. As it turns out, they aren't. The day wears on, and three more smallish fish come aboard. Many others rap the baits momentarily, then shake free.

Unless the weather gets extremely cold in your area, John feels you should be able to catch cats year around. And while natural bait is his overwhelming first choice, Sellers says that blues will occasionally strike artificials. He's caught them up

to 40 pounds while casting bucktail jigs for stripers. At times John has even encountered schools of big cats crashing bait on the surface like stripers or white bass will do. Tossing a shad-imitating lure or white jig into the melee can result in some jarring takes from 10- to 40-pounders.

The wind whips harder as the day grows long. Under the circumstances, Sellers feels fortunate we've landed a 53-pounder plus four smaller cats. But as the sun peeks through the clouds low in the sky and casts a warm orange glow on the lake, a rod throbs violently in its holder and line sizzles off the reel. After fifteen minutes of gut-busting battle, a 44-pounder comes thrashing wildly into Sellers' outstretched net.

Two catfish — together weighing an incredible 97 pounds. After quick photos, the second big cat is freed and lunges back into the murky lake to sulk over its rude encounter.

Where Sellers Finds Catfish in Medium-Depth Reservoirs

Good catfish spots include (A) creek-channel edges, (B) submerged hills and ridges, (C) flooded bridges, (D) old river channels, (E) flooded roadbeds, (F) flooded building foundations, (G) flooded standing timber, (H) sunken islands, (I) saddles between ridges, (J) depressions on a flat bottom, and (K) ditches and canals. These spots produce catfish year around. (NOTE: this is a hypothetical map intended to portray the types of spots Sellers fishes.)

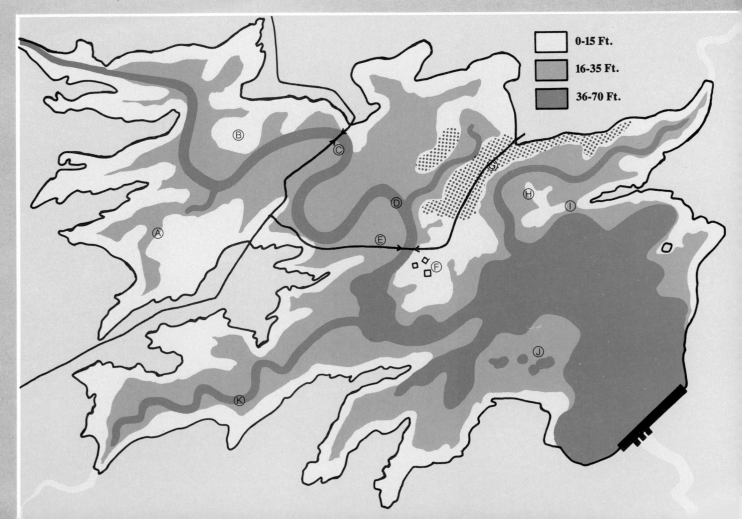

Hot-Air Stripers

by Jake Barnes

Ace guide Jerry Bean uses his little-known balloon-fishing technique to catch magnum stripers

Jerry Bean rummages in his pocket like a ten-year-old looking for a favorite marble, then pulls out a plastic bag of party balloons. He picks a bright orange number and strains to blow it up, until his face matches the color of the bulging rubber. Finally, he knots the inflated balloon around his monofilament line and tosses it overboard.

"Come on, darlin', get out there and work for me," Jerry coos in his Arkansas drawl as he lowers into the water a 15-inch gizzard shad, skewered through the back with a 3/0 hook. Towed by the big shad, the balloon twitches and jerks spasmodically across the water.

Strange, you say: balloons and conversations with bait. You bet it's strange. But in a quiet, understated way, this part-time family farmer and full-time fisherman has set Lake Ouachita abuzz with his success at catching big, battling striped bass.

According to Bean, it all starts with that shad on the end of the line. He treats his bait better than Daddy Warbucks treats Annie. He catches it, cools it, chemicals it, and cajoles it to do its job — which is to be so seductive to the trophy stripers in the lake that they can't resist slurping it down.

This bait-pampering starts in the Arkansas River, 95 miles away, or in shallow, spring-fed arms of Ouachita, where shad seek cool water once the main lake warms in the spring. With a cast net and a great deal of sweaty labor, Jerry collects his prized gizzard shad: a dozen fish on a good throw, or 6 pounds of weed, a bucketload of slime, and an irate turtle on a bad one.

Jerry prefers the shad from the lake for two reasons. First, they're bigger than the river shad. A 15-incher is prime bait; anything under a foot is hardly worth using, although Jerry will put on a

Jerry Bean

Home: *Lonsdale, Arkansas*

Occupation: *Striped bass guide at Lake Ouachita*

Jerry Bean started guiding part-time on Lake Ouachita in the fall of 1982. In the ensuing years he has raised bait fishing to high art — using an unorthodox technique that requires large, wild gizzard shad and ordinary rubber balloons. Jerry won Striper *magazine's striped bass tournament on his home waters in 1985, the first year he entered, and again in 1987. After that initial victory, he started guiding full-time and has gained a reputation for both his fishing skill and his affable manner.*

In 1986 his clients boated five stripers over 40 pounds. The following year the tally was nine fish over 40, including a 47-pound 11-ounce trophy, 5 ounces shy of the lake record. Bean guides and fishes for stripers year around, and catches plenty of big ones himself. Within the next few years, he's determined to break not only the Arkansas state record of 53 pounds, but also the freshwater world record of 60 pounds 8 ounces.

smaller one if the only stripers around are too small to take such behemoths. Second, lake shad are friskier and lighter in color, and Jerry feels a light shad is more visible to the bass.

He transports his haul in a large, insulated, aerated bait tank, which he fills on the spot with cool spring or river water and then treats with rock salt, Bait Saver, and food-grade silicone, the latter to minimize foam buildup. The tank safely holds five to seven dozen shad for three hours.

At his dock Jerry has sunk a 1000-gallon chemical mixing vat, in which he's drilled a scad of 1-inch holes. Here he can keep his shad up to seven weeks. The fish don't eat, but stay frisky with good aeration and a steady flow of fresh spring water from a hose to stabilize temperature. Jerry also has found that after several weeks in the tank the darker river shad will lighten up.

But Jerry's understanding of bait, gained over several years, is only the beginning of his angling success. Even a seductive, lively, 15-inch shad will not draw a strike if just chucked into any old spot. Jerry's maxim of fresh bait over a big fish means the fisherman must know where the big fish hide.

And hide they do. Contrary to the popular notion that stripers are cruising fish, constantly on the move in search of a meal, Jerry believes they seek the cover of deep water and hold there when not on a feed — particularly in an impoundment like Lake Ouachita with its submerged, heavily timbered ridges and valleys.

There is no simple means of finding where the stripers hold. Like anything else worthwhile, it takes effort and hours. A fisherman must cruise the lake in the morning and evening to look for bass feeding on the surface and to graph the valleys that

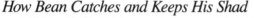

How Bean Catches and Keeps His Shad

CAST-NET in shallow water to catch shad. Tie the rope to your wrist and with the same hand, grasp the net where it attaches to the rope. Hold the lead line with your teeth and other hand. Throw with a sidearm motion.

TRANSPORT shad in a tank filled with cool water where shad are caught. Bean's boat tank is insulated and aerated.

KEEP shad in a large tank for long-term storage. Bean uses a big mixing vat drilled with holes.

156

offer cover, especially near points, ridges, flats, and creeks which attract bait.

At times when there's a thermocline, the stripers generally are found just below it or anywhere on down to the bottom. With no thermocline, they tend to stay deeper if the sun is bright or boat traffic is heavy; they stay shallower on dull days with little disturbance from boats.

Sometimes Bean trolls jigs or plugs to locate the fish, then switches to the balloons. He often trolls with a spreader rig made from an 18-inch length of wire. His favorite source is heater-vent cable from old Chevrolets. To each end of the wire he attaches a 30- to 36-inch section of mono; to its middle, a third section 6 inches longer. The lures attached to these are 7-inch minnow plugs, or 1- to 2-ounce bucktail jigs with 5- to 7-inch twister-tail or curly-tail trailers. Bean feels that spreader rigs are more

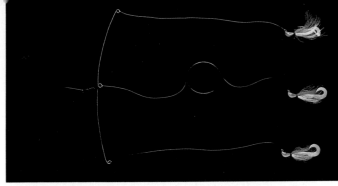

Bean's spreader rig

effective than a single lure because they resemble a baitfish school. He trolls two spreader rigs at once, either flat-lined or fished on downriggers.

Bean has found a number of spots on Ouachita that regularly hold stripers in summer. One of his favorites is a valley 80 feet deep with standing timber 50 feet high. Here the fish hide during the day; they feed on a large nearby flat, 10 to 12 feet deep, in the morning and evening, and after dark.

Bean's deck boat allows unobstructed fishing off bow, sides, stern

Bean likes to leave the dock about 5:00 a.m. When he's guiding a full party of four anglers — a comfortable number on his 22½-foot Hurricane deck boat, he carries up to five dozen shad in his bait tank. As the day warms, he'll slip some ice into the insulated tank to keep the water cool and the shad frisky.

Checking contours, charting stripers

Zigzagging over the valley, Jerry will often chart stripers on his paper graph recorder or his LCR. If nothing shows, there's still a good chance fish will move into the valley during the day as they return from feeding. Bean anchors upwind of the valley, using a cement block rather than a navy anchor so as not to snag in the timber, and then he rigs up. He uses tackle that affords dependability plus good sport: 7½-foot flipping rods, heavy-duty baitcasting reels spooled with 15- or 20-pound mono, and carefully sharpened 3/0 hooks.

He wants the bait to suspend 10 feet above the timber, where stripers lurking in the treetops can see it above them and, as is their habit, chase the bait to the surface. Measuring his line against his rod, he strips off about three lengths — 21 feet — and ties on a balloon. With an average 12-inch shad, he'll inflate the balloon to the size of a softball; larger bait demands a bigger balloon. He then ties a simple overhand knot in the neck of the balloon to attach it to the line. In the evening, he'll often slip a Cyalume Light Stick into the balloon to increase its visibility.

There is logic in this order of events. He used to bait the hook first, and then tie on the balloon — until the time a 40-pounder rolled up while he was rigging and inhaled the shad next to the boat, nearly garroting his lips, fingers, and nose.

Jerry starts talking to the bait as soon as it hits the water. If some headstrong shad does not want to swim toward the valley of stripers, he can direct it by carefully holding back until it points in the right direction, then giving line. When the bait is 100 feet from the boat, he flips on the clicker but keeps the reel in freespool. The clicker is enough to keep the shad within striking range. If the bait goes much beyond 100 feet, the elasticity of the line makes it difficult to set the hook on a big fish; any closer, though, and the boat may spook the fish.

The balloon cuts a neat *V* across the water as the shad swims away. Unlike smaller bait, these big shad actually work an area, cutting back and forth looking for their own kind and for shelter from the jaws beneath. Jerry usually fishes two rods at once; he gives the baits thirty minutes to work at the end of their tethers.

How to Rig Shad for Ballooning

STRETCH neck of balloon and tie on line with overhand knot. Position so bait swims at desired depth.

INSERT 3/0 hook just ahead of the dorsal fin. Do not use a sinker; it will restrict the shad too much.

LOWER rig into water and let shad swim off. Casting could tear shad from hook and may kill it.

If nothing happens, he eases up the anchor and lets the wind gently push the boat toward the stripers' lair. When necessary, he corrects his course with a trolling motor. Back and forth the shad swim.

This is where the balloon demonstrates its superiority to a bobber. A balloon controls the bait without inhibiting its natural movement; unlike a bobber, it stays completely above the surface and allows the shad to swim freely from side to side. In addition, the balloon is so big it's easy to spot in the glare on the water 30 to 40 yards away. And when a fish hits, the balloon either breaks immediately or slides down the line as the striper runs for deep water.

Who first came up with the balloon idea is anyone's guess. Jerry started using balloons to fish commercially for catfish a number of years ago. He may have been the one to introduce them to striper fishermen on Ouachita, but he can't say for sure. If he wasn't, he certainly helped popularize their use.

In the stern are two rods rigged with 7-inch floating Cotton Cordell Red Fins, proven striper lures, in case a fish breaks water within casting range. More often than not, however, any striper thrashing through the neighborhood will be attracted to those luscious shad.

And it's not hard to tell when a big fish is somewhere nearby. A shad is nothing more than a swimming care-package, and the shad knows it. When a striper approaches, the shad panics and the balloon is

Where Bean Finds Striped Bass in Deep Reservoirs

In November and December, stripers are found at depths of 15 to 25 feet on (A) long points extending into the old river channel in the upper end of the lake and on (B) main-lake points that form coves. In January and February, small to medium-sized stripers move farther up the old river channel, stopping at (C) the last hole with at least 50 feet of water. They swim into the river itself at night, spawning over shallow shoals, but return to the holes the next morning. Large stripers may spawn in (D) short, steep coves along the old river channel. After spawning, all the stripers begin moving back down the lake. Bean finds them along (E) the edges of shallow flats where shad spawn. From May through July, stripers suspend over (F) old creek channels, or in submerged timber along their edges. In summer they hang just below the thermocline, which forms at 28 to 32 feet; they move shallower at dawn and dusk, feeding on nearby flats from 8 to 12 feet deep. During the day, Bean fishes just above the thermocline. If you lower a shad below the thermocline, the temperature change will kill it. Stripers are deeper from August through mid-September, suspending in (G) deep river channels in the lower end of the lake. They still hang just below the thermocline, which now forms at 35 to 45 feet, but some are as deep as 75 feet. Again, Bean fishes just above the thermocline. The fall turnover occurs from mid-September through October. Stripers scatter and can be found almost anywhere. The most likely spot is near (H) the junction of a creek channel and the main river channel, at depths of about 25 feet. Beginning at the turnover and continuing into April, there is some surface feeding, especially in morning and evening.

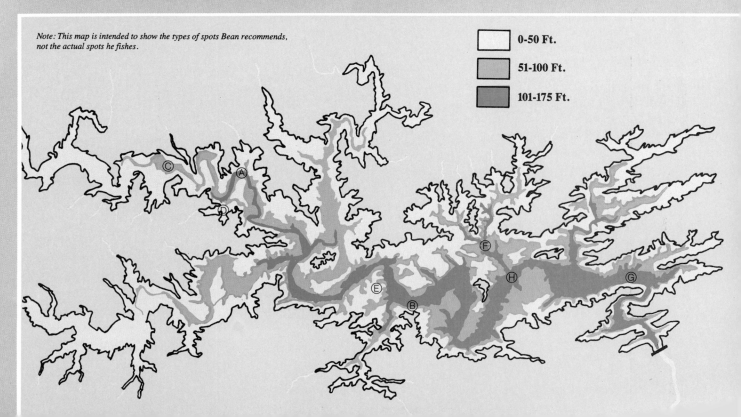

Note: This map is intended to show the types of spots Bean recommends, not the actual spots he fishes.

	0-50 Ft.
	51-100 Ft.
	101-175 Ft.

towed about, shaking and skittering like a waterskier at an alligator farm.

A big striper will hit in one of two ways. It may ambush the bait underwater, in which case the balloon will burst or slide up the line. The angler need only set the hook and brace himself. But sometimes the bass chases the shad to the surface, and the shad thrashes around in an attempt to escape. Here the fisherman has to show some patience and allow the bass to catch the shad and swim off with it before setting the hook.

When a big 15-inch shad starts towing his balloon, Jerry gets ready. He picks the rod out of its holder, flicks off the clicker, and waits. Suddenly, the water boils. The bait jumps out of the water. The water churns again, and the dorsal fin of a bass is barely visible. The bait, now in shock, flutters and trembles on the surface. The bass turns and sucks it down.

Jerry quickly takes up slack in the line, then lets the fish run. When he's sure it's taken the bait, he engages the reel and sets the hook. The bass turns toward the boat, screeches within 30 feet, makes a hard right turn and peels off 200 feet of line. Jerry manages to turn the fish. Working hard to keep it out of the timber below, he recovers all the line he lost.

Soon the fish is next to the boat, then aboard. It's a 30-pound striper — not immense by Jerry Bean's standards, but certainly impressive by anyone else's.

"Just like crappie fishing," he says. "You run out some bait, watch the bobber, then reel them in."

He cracks a big grin.

Bean's 30-pounder